TRULY HEALTHY VEGAN COOKBOOK

Truly Healthy
VEGAN
COOKBOOK

90 WHOLE-FOOD RECIPES WITH DELICIOUSLY SIMPLE INGREDIENTS

DIANNE WENZ

Photography by Antonis Achilleos

ROCKRIDGE
PRESS

For general information on our other products and services or to obtain technical support, please contact our Customer Care Department within the United States at (866) 744-2665, or outside the United States at (510) 253-0500.

Rockridge Press publishes its books in a variety of electronic and print formats. Some content that appears in print may not be available in electronic books, and vice versa.

Interior & Cover Designer: Erin Yeung
Art Producer: Karen Williams
Editor: Michael Goodman
Production Editor: Matthew Burnett

Photography © 2019 Antonis Achilleos. Food styling by Rishion Hannes. Prop styling by Mindi Shapiro. Author photo courtesy of © Dennis Mason

ISBN: Print 978-1-64611-227-2 | eBook 978-1-64611-228-9

R0

For the animals.

CONTENTS

INTRODUCTION

When I went vegetarian in 1992, there were not very many ready-made vegetarian foods available. There was one brand of veggie burger available at my local grocery store, and it tasted slightly like the cardboard box it was packaged in. Dairy-free cheeses resembled waxy blocks of melted crayons.

Eating out in restaurants was a chore back then. Vegetarian options were usually limp iceberg lettuce salads drowning in vinegar alongside a plate of oily French fries. I remember once going out to eat with my family, and salad was not even an option. Instead, I had a plate of spaghetti with marinara sauce and a dry baked potato.

Thankfully, things have changed so much since then! Restaurants and fast food chains are adding meatless options to their menus. There is now an abundance of delicious vegan products available at just about any market. And there are countless brands of veggie burgers and dairy-free cheeses that will actually melt.

However, simply because a food is free of meat, eggs, and dairy products doesn't mean it's good for you. There is a common misconception that "vegan" and "healthy" are synonyms. For instance, those "healthy" packages of dairy-free cheese and meatless meats are heavily processed and usually lacking in nutrients. I once baked sugary, oil-filled cupcakes for someone and the next time I saw her, she remarked at how amazing it was that something so sinful could be good for you. I didn't have the heart to tell her that those cupcakes were actually fat-filled calorie-bombs.

A few years after going vegetarian, I decided to remove dairy and eggs from my diet, too, and the chronic headaches and sinusitis that had been plaguing me my whole life cleared up in just a few short weeks. Because of my own experience, I developed an interest in healing through food, and I wanted to spread my knowledge to anyone who would listen.

And I really wanted to help all those people who would tell me, "I tried to go vegan once, but I got sick," or "I would like to give up meat, but I need my protein." I also wanted to help those who did not know what to cook and would end up having pasta or frozen veggie burgers for dinner every night.

I became a health coach so I could help people go vegan and I became a chef so I could teach them how to cook healthy, plant-based meals. The *Truly Healthy Vegan Cookbook* is a condensed, handheld version of being my client. Throughout the book, I'll share my tips and tricks with you, along with some of my favorite healthy recipes.

I have heard people say that they are vegan for the animals and not for their health, so they don't care if they eat junk food. But why not be both? You can care about the animals and take care of yourself at the same time. So, in this book, I will also be sharing recipes for healthy, veganized versions of comfort food favorites, such as burgers, tacos, and macaroni and cheese.

CHAPTER ONE

THE HEALTHY VEGAN

Following a healthy vegan diet can be difficult. One of the most common comments I hear is, "I want to go vegan, but I'm not sure what to eat." Some people think that once they go vegan, they can't eat anything but "rabbit food." Others swap the packaged, processed foods they are used to eating with packaged, processed vegan versions of the same thing. People have also told me that they think it might be too expensive because they'll need to purchase so many specialty ingredients and additional, fancy kitchen equipment.

Of course, practicing vegans who know what to eat can run into issues, too. It can be tough for those who live with family members who are not vegan. Meal planning and juggling the dietary needs of others takes time. And many find it tricky to just get a hot, home-cooked meal on the table after a long day of work.

Meatless Is Not Enough

Many people think that simply eliminating meat and cheese from their diets means they're eating healthy, but that's not necessarily the case. There are plenty of vegan foods that are loaded with processed sugars, white flour, and unhealthy fats—and they all fall flat when it comes to nutrition.

An Unhealthy Vegan Diet

This is a great time to be vegan! Animal-free versions of everything from eggs and cheese to burgers and meatballs are available in just about any grocery store. Many snack foods and candies are technically vegan, too. Unfortunately, most of them are made with highly processed ingredients such as soy protein isolate, white flour, and white sugar—or come loaded with way too much oil.

With all the ingredients that are now readily available, it's possible to make vegan versions of just about anything you can imagine, including pepperoni pizza, chocolate cake, and cream-filled donuts. Now, don't get me wrong—I will eat those foods (I rarely pass up a slice of vegan chocolate cake!), but they're once-in-a-while things, not mainstays of my diet.

Those types of foods have their place, but they shouldn't be a regular part of the daily menu. A diet that relies heavily on packaged, processed foods with added sugars and fats falls short nutritionally and is not sustainable for maintaining one's long-term health.

In my health coaching practice, I sometimes see vegan clients who don't eat many vegetables. It can be easy to go through an entire day and consume very little fresh produce. Here's an example of an unhealthy vegan diet over the course of a day:

- A bowl of cereal with soy milk for breakfast.

- A meatless "turkey" and nondairy cheese sandwich on white bread with a side of potato chips for lunch.

- A few cookies and a mug of sugary coffee for an afternoon pick-me-up.

- White pasta with marinara and meatless "meatballs" for dinner, sprinkled with nondairy Parmesan cheese.

- A bowl of nondairy ice cream for dessert.

While those meals are free of animal ingredients, they are full of empty calories and don't contain many nutrients.

TOP 10 VEGAN DIET MISTAKES

Since going vegan is a totally new way of living, it can be easy to make some mistakes in the beginning. It's important to not beat yourself up and just learn from the experience. Here are some common dietary mistakes I see new vegans make:

Eating too many vegan meats and cheeses. We tend to reach for foods that are familiar, so if chicken parmesan was an omnivore favorite, you might be tempted to cook meatless "chicken" smothered in nondairy cheese.

Not eating enough vegetables. With the abundance of vegan packaged and processed foods available today, it's super easy to overlook real vegetables. However, they should really be front and center on the plate.

Not eating leafy greens. Leafy greens are so nutritious they should be their own food group. They're loaded with vitamins and minerals, including calcium, so include them in as many meals as you can.

Not eating enough food. People have told me they tried to go vegan, but they were hungry all the time. It turned out that they weren't eating enough. Foods like vegetables and beans aren't as caloric as meats and cheeses, so you need to eat more of them.

Eating too much pasta. It's easy to become a pasta-tarian when eating meatless. Pasta is easy to make, and it's often vegan. But a lot of it is made with white flour and doesn't contain many nutrients.

Filling up on empty calories. Many packaged, processed foods are vegan, but most are severely lacking in nutrients and high in calories.

Not planning ahead. Meal planning is key for sticking to a nutritious diet. Make sure healthy snacks and meals are available when traveling, too.

CONTINUED

Making a Vegan Diet Healthy

The word "healthy" is open to interpretation. One person's definition of a healthy diet can vary greatly from someone else's. For me, a healthy diet is one that's full of whole, unprocessed foods. It should include nutrient-dense foods like leafy greens; fresh vegetables; whole grains; and protein-rich beans, nuts, and seeds.

What Is Healthy?

In this book, I offer a whole-foods approach to healthy meals with a focus on balancing nutritional needs. If you're not 100 percent committed to healthy eating, that's totally okay. The vegan police won't break down your door and demand you eat a kale salad if you have one bag of potato chips. There's always a place for an occasional decadent meal or dessert—as long as you remember that being free of eggs and butter doesn't make that slice of cake a healthy treat.

We're all human, so it's impossible to totally avoid illnesses, but eating a whole-food, plant-based diet has been shown to boost the immune system and ward off non-infectious diseases, such as heart disease, diabetes, and certain cancers. Eating this way can also increase energy and decrease aches and pains. Keep in mind that there might be an adjustment period, so you may feel tired or achy as your body gets used to this new diet.

Heavy on Whole Foods

The recipes in this cookbook focus on whole, unprocessed foods. Whole foods include vegetables, fruits, nuts, seeds, legumes, and whole grains. Whole grains are those that have their endosperm, germ, and bran attached and include brown rice, wheat, barley, and oats. Quinoa, amaranth, and buckwheat are usually included in lists of whole grains, but they're actually pseudo-cereals or seeds.

People are sometimes confused about what is and isn't a whole food, especially when it comes to carbohydrates and grains. I blame the advertising industry for that. A few years ago, whole grains were all the rage, and you couldn't turn on the TV without seeing commercials for sugar-laden breakfast cereals "made with whole grains." Sure, the raw ingredients started out as whole grains, but they were processed into an unrecognizable state, with their nutrients stripped out along the way. Oats are whole grains, and they're a better breakfast option.

To figure out if something is a whole food or not, check the packaging. If it came in a box with a long list of ingredients you can't pronounce, it's not a whole food. If it came unwrapped or in a simple container with just a few ingredients listed, chances are that it's a whole food.

When buying products like bread or pasta, avoid white, flour-based products, and look for whole grains listed as the main ingredients. Protein-based pastas made with chickpeas and lentils are good choices for those with gluten and wheat sensitivities.

Balancing Act

While most omnivores tend to make their meals very protein-heavy, those on a meat-free diet sometimes fill their plates with carbohydrates like bread, pasta, or white rice. While I don't follow a low-carb diet and this isn't a low-carb cookbook, I recommend staying away from processed, simple carbohydrates and focusing instead on complex carbohydrates like legumes and whole grains—and, of course, vegetables.

Because meat-free meals usually lack the focus of a central protein, new vegans can find it tricky to put together a meal. My advice: Don't worry about what should be at the center of the plate. Instead, focus on including a variety of nutrient-dense foods.

Vegetables should be the main component of a meal, and I recommend including a variety of different-colored veggies for each meal because they contain different kinds of healthy compounds known as phytonutrients. Green should always be one of the colors included on a plate because leafy green vegetables are loaded with vitamins and minerals. Leafy greens also tend to be the one food that's most lacking in our diets.

When putting together a meal, half of the plate should be vegetables. A source of carbohydrates, such as whole grains, should take up about a quarter of it. The other quarter should contain a protein source, such as beans, tofu, or tempeh. This doesn't mean you have to precisely measure your food—just estimate it.

SUPPLEMENTS TO CONSIDER

While I advocate for a nutrient-dense diet, it can still be difficult to get all the vitamins and minerals we need from our diets. A few of these are almost impossible to get from a vegan diet (and no, they're not protein and calcium). I take these supplements and I recommend them to my health coaching clients as well:

Vitamin B12. It's pretty much impossible to get this vitamin from plants. Although it is found in some fortified food, most nutrition experts recommend a supplement. Our bodies store B12 for years, so it can take a while for a deficiency to develop, but it's important to prevent that from happening. In his book *How Not to Die*, Michael Greger, MD, recommends that adults under the age of 65 take 2,500 micrograms of vitamin B12 each week. Because it can be difficult for the body to absorb it as we grow older, he recommends that adults over age 65 increase their intake to 1,000 micrograms a day.

Vitamin D. A vitamin D supplement is one that everyone, not just vegans, should consider taking. This nutrient doesn't come from food; it's a compound we produce after our skin is exposed to direct sunlight. Matching the right amount of sunlight for your skin tone at the right time of day where you live can be tricky, so supplementing can be important. The USDA recommended daily allowance of vitamin D for adults is 600 international units (IU), but many experts recommend taking 2,000 IU.

Iodine. This mineral is important for thyroid function, and it's found primarily in seafood, dairy milk, and iodized salt. It can also be found in sea vegetables, so consider adding them to your diet if you don't want to supplement. If you choose to supplement, Brenda Davis, RD, and Vesanto Melina, MS, RD, recommend taking 150 micrograms per day in their book *Becoming Vegan*. Be careful not to take too much, as it can cause goiters.

Omega-3 fatty acids. There are two kinds of omega-3s: short chain and long chain. Short-chain alpha-linolenic acid (ALA) fatty acids are found in flax and chia seeds, while long-chain eicosapentaenoic acid (EPA) and docosahexaenoic acid (DHA) fatty acids are primarily found in fish. Dr. Greger recommends taking 250 milligrams of yeast- or algae-derived omega-3s to ensure we're getting everything we need.

Always talk to your doctor before taking any new supplement. It's a good idea to get a blood test, especially when starting a new diet, to make sure your nutritional needs are being met.

Planning and Prepping

Planning and prepping make cooking and eating easier. Otherwise, it gets too easy to hit up the snack machine for a bag of potato chips or stop at the pizza place for dinner on the way home. Planning your whole week of meals ahead of time can be helpful, but it can be just as beneficial simply to plan your lunch or dinner earlier in the day.

Meal planning saves money. If you make a grocery list and stick to it, you're less likely to buy food on a whim. It's also cheaper to cook at home than to order take-out night after night. Planning ahead can be less wasteful, too. You're less likely to let vegetables languish and rot in the produce drawer if you know how you're going to cook them.

Many of us come home tired each evening, and we'd rather spend time with our families than in the kitchen. Prepping foods ahead makes our time in the kitchen more productive and helps us get dinner on the table quickly.

You might think that prepping ahead of time will take up half of your precious weekend, but that's not necessarily the case. Sure, you can cook all of your meals ahead of time and store them in containers in the refrigerator, but meal prepping can be as simple as batch cooking grains or beans or chopping vegetables as soon as you get home from the grocery store.

The Healthy Vegan Pantry

I often hear people mistakenly referring to protein, fat, and carbohydrates as food groups, but they're not—they are macronutrients. Macronutrients are the parts of food that provide calories, and they're essential for the body to function. Most foods, except those that are highly processed, are a combination of two or three macronutrients.

Protein Power

People often say they could never go vegan because "I need my protein." I assure you that there is plenty of protein in the world of plant foods. In fact, most omnivores are probably consuming too much protein, which can lead to a host of health problems.

Of the 20 amino acids that are comprised within protein, our body can synthesize 11 of them. Therefore, we need to get the other nine, known as essential amino acids, from other types of food.

Protein is the building block of life, and it's essential for the body's structural and mechanical functions. The recommended daily allowance (RDA) is 0.8 gram of protein per kilogram (2.2 pounds) of bodyweight for the average adult. So, a person who weighs 150 pounds would need to consume around 61 grams of protein, which is pretty easy to accomplish on a vegan diet.

(Note: Children, pregnant and nursing mothers, and athletes have different needs, depending on their circumstances.)

Some of my favorite sources of protein include:

Tofu. This incredibly versatile protein can be used in many different types of meals. Half a cup contains 10 grams of protein.

Tempeh. This is a traditional Indonesian food made from whole, fermented soybeans, and it's much heartier than tofu. Half a cup contains 15 grams of protein.

Seitan. This protein is made with wheat, and it has a hearty, meaty texture. One serving of seitan (1/3 cup) contains 21 grams of protein.

Chickpeas. These can be added as-is to salads and stews, roasted and eaten as a snack, or blended with tahini and lemon juice for a delicious dip. Half a cup of chickpeas contains about 14 grams of protein.

Lentils. These quick-cooking legumes have a meaty texture, and they can be used in everything from burgers to soups. Half a cup contains 12 grams of protein.

Peas. Peas are actually seeds, and they make a great addition to soups, casseroles, and salads. Half a cup contains four grams of protein.

Quinoa. Yes, quinoa is often thought of as a carbohydrate, not a protein, but it's possible to be both! When cooked, half a cup has four grams of protein, and it contains all nine essential amino acids.

Hemp seeds. Like quinoa, hemp seeds contain all nine essential amino acids. In fact, hemp seeds contain all 20 aminos. Just one tablespoon contains three grams of protein.

Additionally, many other protein sources exist. All beans, nuts, and seeds have it, and even leafy greens, potatoes, and brown rice contain significant amounts of protein.

Healthy Fats

Healthy fats provide the body with fatty acids, which it can't generate itself and are necessary to absorb certain vitamins.

Monounsaturated fats are fatty acids that contain one double bond in their structure. They're found in olives, peanuts, almonds, and avocados, as well as within their oils. These oils are liquid at room temperature and will turn cloudy and thicken up when refrigerated.

Polyunsaturated fats contain at least two double bonds in their structure. They're found in walnuts, flaxseeds, hempseeds, chia seeds, and vegetable oils. Polyunsaturated oils are liquid at room temperature and stay liquid in the refrigerator.

Omega-3 fatty acids are a type of polyunsaturated fat. They can reduce inflammation and protect the brain. They also regulate the immune system and are needed for the nervous system to function properly. Short-chain ALA omega-3 fatty acids can be found in soy, leafy green vegetables, and walnuts, as well as chia, hemp, and flax seeds. Long-chain EPA and DHA aren't found in plant-based foods, and they should be supplemented (see page 6).

My favorite sources of healthy fats include:

Avocados. Smooth and buttery, they're great on everything from toast to tacos.

Tahini. This paste made from ground sesame seeds has a variety of uses. I like to make salad dressing with it, but it's also a great addition to sauces, smoothies, and soups.

Cashews. These little nuts are pretty magical. They can be blended with water to make "cream." Add a few more ingredients, and you have a delicious, dairy-free cheese. They can be used to make dairy-free ice cream, sauces, and even milk. And, of course, they're a terrific snack.

Olives. I used to hate olives, but now I can't get enough. I like to toss them into salads or snack on them with a handful of almonds. They can also be used to make delicious tapenade.

Chia seeds. When mixed with a liquid, chia seeds thicken and gel, so they can be used as an egg replacer when baking. They're commonly used to make pudding, but they can be used in jams, breads, and oatmeal.

Complex Carbs

Carbohydrates have been getting a bad rap lately, but they're vital for fueling the brain, nervous system, and red blood cells. They also come in many forms, and not all of them are created equal. Part of the problem is that whole foods, like brown rice and chickpeas, and processed foods, like donuts and potato chips, are all categorized as "carbs."

Refined carbohydrates are found in abundance in processed foods like cakes, crackers, white bread, and breakfast cereals. They may fill you up, but they have little to no nutritional value.

Simple carbohydrates contain one or two saccharides—or sugar—molecules. They can be found in fruits and non-starchy vegetables, like cucumbers and peppers, but they're also found in sugars and sweeteners.

Complex carbohydrates are also called polysaccharides because they contain three or more sugar molecules. They are found in whole grains, beans, sweet potatoes, corn, and beets. These foods help you feel full, staving off the urge to snack.

Unrefined, complex carbohydrates include starches and fiber, which have many health benefits. A 2019 study published in *The Lancet* that was commissioned by the World Health Organization showed that consuming between 25 and 29 grams of fiber is ideal for optimal health and preventing chronic diseases such as heart disease, type 2 diabetes, and certain cancers.

The recipes in this book will contain complex carbohydrates, and I'll even share some recipes for vegetable-based alternatives, like cauliflower rice and zucchini noodles.

Putting It All Together

In this cookbook, I will share some of my favorite healthy recipes. You can follow them to the letter or adjust them to suit your own tastes. It's possible to make meals from some of the basics that I share, and I encourage you to mix and match your favorite components from the recipes.

If you don't feel like following an exact recipe, you can easily put together a quick and easy meal using ingredients you probably already have on hand. Most of us already have beans and grains—all you need to do is add a vegetable or two and some spices, and you'll have a quick and easy meal!

Consider these options:

- With half a container of leftover brown rice, a diced tomato, a few chopped romaine lettuce leaves, and a can of beans, you can quickly make a burrito bowl. Add a little hot sauce to heat things up.

- A container of vegetable stock, a can of chickpeas, a little minced garlic, and a few handfuls of chopped greens can be thrown together to make a healthy soup.

- Beans, diced tomatoes, vegetable stock, chopped vegetables, and chili powder can be combined to make chili.

Kitchen Equipment

It can be difficult to adjust to a new way of eating while learning how to prepare meals from scratch. Having kitchen equipment on hand can make prep and cooking times much easier.

Must Have

Chances are you already have most, if not all, of the things on my must-have list. They're essential to all types of cooking—not just for vegan food.

Sharp knife. A good, sharp knife is necessary for any kitchen, especially one where a lot of vegetable chopping takes place. The right knife will feel comfortable in your hand, and you will enjoy using it. It's best to shop for knives at a store that'll allow you to handle them.

Cutting board. If you're going to be chopping veggies, you'll need a cutting board. I like to use a plastic board because it can go in the dishwasher. If your cutting board is wooden, take care to wash it well because it can harbor bacteria.

Stockpot. A large pot is essential for soups, stews, and pastas.

Sauté pan. I use a 12-inch stainless steel pan to cook most of the meals in my kitchen. It's great for stir-frying as well as sautéing.

Cast-iron pan. A well-seasoned cast-iron pan will act like a non-stick skillet, making it easy to cook with little to no oil.

Baking dish. I love making lasagnas and casseroles, especially in the cooler months, and a 9-by-13-inch dish is essential for baking them.

Baking sheets. Baking sheets, or sheet pans, are essential in not only roasting and baking vegetables, but also for baking cookies.

Blender. Blenders are essential for making smoothies, dressings, and creamy soups.

Box grater. Grating vegetables is an excellent way to hide them in dishes. It can also add a different texture to your meals.

Nice to Have

It's not necessary to have fancy equipment to make a delicious vegan meal, but sometimes it helps speed things up. Some of my recipes may call for these gadgets, but I will give an alternative way to prepare foods for those who don't have them handy.

Food processor. I don't know how I coped before I had a food processor. It can grate, slice, and mix in a matter of seconds.

High-speed blender. A regular blender can mix soups and sauces, but a high-speed blender can do the job in a flash. It can also be used to easily blend nuts into milks and creams.

Spiralizer. It does just what the name suggests—it turns vegetables into spiral, pasta-like strips.

Air fryer. I was skeptical before I bought my air fryer but, after using it once or twice, I became a believer. It cooks most foods in half the time it would take in an oven, and it doesn't heat up the kitchen the way an oven does.

Slow cooker. Having one of these is wonderful because you can put the ingredients for your meal in it in the morning and come home from work to a prepared, hot meal. I love using mine in the summer because I can cook a meal in it without heating up the kitchen.

Mandoline slicer. One of these is handy because it can slice vegetables paper-thin. It also can grate and julienne.

Immersion blender. This gadget can be used to blend soups and sauces right in the pot, creating less of a mess than your upright blender.

About the Recipes

The recipes in this book will provide you with meals that are truly healthy and satisfying. They're all made with whole foods, and I've kept nutritional balance in mind while creating them. Since they're vegan, they don't contain any meat, eggs, or dairy products.

Many of these recipes contain whole grains and beans, which are integral to a vegan diet, but they're not necessarily the star of the dish. In most cases, vegetables are the main focus of the meal. I've snuck in extra veggies wherever I could, and I'm guessing that picky eaters won't even notice them.

To make prepping meals as easy as possible, many of the recipes will take 30 minutes or less, some will contain no more than five ingredients, and others will require just one main piece of equipment, such as a pot, skillet, or sheet pan.

Be sure to note the recipe yield for each dish. Each recipe will list the yield as well as nutritional information per serving. If a recipe serves six and you eat half of it, you may have eaten healthy food, but you've eaten too much of it. The section on quick snacks (see page 12) will help stave off the munchies if a dish's proper portion leaves you feeling a little hungry.

I know that not everyone is going to go vegan overnight, and I also know that cooking for families with mixed dietary needs can be tricky. Some of you may be in need of easy Meatless Monday meals or dishes that can be adapted to your family's tastes. If you want to go fully vegan or are looking for easy healthy meals to add into your flexitarian diet, I am here to help.

For those who are watching their carbohydrate intake, you'll notice that some recipes will be marked "low-carb." These dishes contain no more than 30 grams of carbohydrates. Recipe labels will also note if a recipe is gluten-free, nut-free, soy-free, or oil-free.

Oil is a touchy subject in the healthy food world. Some experts will tell you to avoid it altogether, while others will say it's okay in moderation. Some will say that coconut oil is the best kind to cook with because it can't go rancid, but others will tell you to avoid it at all costs because it's a saturated fat.

Oil is pure fat and high in calories (one tablespoon contains 120 calories). So, when it is used, it should be done in moderation. I don't follow an oil-free diet, and I use a little in my recipes. I like to cook with avocado oil, which has a neutral flavor and doesn't go bad as easily as more delicate oils like extra-virgin olive oil. If you follow an oil-free diet, you can omit the oil from the recipes or substitute water or vegetable stock.

After each recipe, you'll find some handy tips. They include:

Ingredient tip. More information on an ingredient, from its versatility or where to look for it in the grocery store.

Substitution tip. Ideas on how to swap ingredients—for seasonality, to create a different flavor profile, or because of allergies.

Make-ahead tip. Some recipes or recipe components can be made ahead of time and reheated at mealtime.

Prep tip. Advice on preparing a recipe's ingredients.

Speed it up. In a hurry? Some recipes have shortcuts, like using a food processor for prep work or an air fryer for faster cooking.

Slow it down. If you have more time on your hands, some recipes can be cooked in a slow cooker or simmered on the stovetop for longer periods of time.

I hope you're hungry because I'm super excited to share my healthy vegan recipes with you. For many people, the term "healthy food" conjures up images of boring, bland meals. That's not the case here. These dishes are packed with flavor and sure to satisfy. Let's get into the kitchen and start cooking!

ALLERGY ALERT: HOW TO SWAP INGREDIENTS

Food allergies and conditions like celiac disease can make it difficult to cook recipes as they are written. Some common food allergies and sensitivities include gluten, wheat, nuts, and soy. Here are some suggestions for ingredient substitution:

Gluten and wheat. Brown rice or quinoa can be substituted for grains that contain gluten, such as barley. Instead of whole-wheat flour, use a gluten-free flour mix, such as Bob's Red Mill 1-to-1 Baking Flour. Gluten-free bread or tortillas can be used to make sandwiches, or a collard leaf can be used to make a wrap. Instead of soy sauce, use a wheat-free tamari or Bragg Liquid Aminos.

Nuts and nut butters. Sunflower seed butter, soy nut butter, and tahini can easily be swapped for nut butters. Seeds, such as pumpkin or sunflower, can be used in place of nuts.

Soy. Instead of tofu or tempeh, almost any type of bean can be used. Chickpeas make a nice substitute for tofu, and lentils have a hearty texture that is similar to tempeh. If you're not sensitive to gluten, seitan can be used. Coconut aminos can be used instead of soy sauce or tamari.

Fruits. Bananas and avocados can be allergens for some. Applesauce can sometimes be used instead of bananas. In salads, avocado can be omitted or replaced with beans or nuts. If you're not allergic to both, bananas can sometimes be swapped for avocados, and vice versa.

CHAPTER TWO

BASICS

HOMEMADE VEGETABLE STOCK

GLUTEN-FREE | LOW-CARB | NUT-FREE | OIL-FREE | SOY-FREE

MAKES about 4 cups | PREP TIME: 10 minutes | COOK TIME: 1 hour

Most store-bought stocks are high in sodium, so I like to make my own. Stock is the building block for soup, and it can infuse flavor into many recipes, including sauces, dressings, and even stir-fries. This can be adapted to suit whatever vegetables you have on hand. Leeks can be used in place of onions, and mushrooms can be added to the mixture. I like to add vegetable scraps, so they don't go to waste.

5 cups water

2 carrots, chopped

3 celery stalks, chopped

1 onion, chopped

1 tomato, chopped

3 garlic cloves

¼ cup fresh parsley

1 bay leaf

1. Combine water, carrots, celery, onion, tomato, garlic, parsley, and bay leaf in a large stockpot. Bring to a boil and then lower to a simmer. Let simmer for 1 hour, and then remove from heat.

2. Cool for 12 to 20 minutes.

3. Place a strainer or colander over a large bowl and pour the stock into the strainer, allowing the liquid to collect in the bowl.

4. Use immediately or place in an airtight container in the refrigerator or freezer.

Slow it down: If you're not in a hurry, combine the ingredients in a slow cooker and cook on low for 6 to 8 hours.

Per serving (1 cup): Calories: 15; Total fat: 0g; Total carbs: 4g; Fiber: 0g; Sugar: 1g; Protein: 0g; Sodium: 62mg

ZUCCHINI NOODLES

GLUTEN-FREE | LOW-CARB | NUT-FREE | OIL-FREE | SOY-FREE

SERVES 4 | PREP TIME: 40 minutes | COOK TIME: 5 minutes

Zucchini noodles, or "zoodles," started out as a secret among raw vegans, but word quickly spread to carb-conscious vegans and those with gluten sensitivities. They've become so popular that you can now buy frozen, pre-packed zucchini noodles in just about any grocery store. However, fresh zucchini noodles are extremely easy to make at home. Toss these noodles in your favorite pasta sauce and dinner is ready.

2 large zucchinis (or yellow
  summer squash)
1 teaspoon sea salt

Substitution tip: Zucchini and summer squash are not the only sources for great noodle options. Other vegetables can be turned into noodles, too. Try making them with beets, sweet potatoes, carrots, parsnips, and butternut squash. You can skip the salting step if you're using one of these hearty vegetables (since they're not as watery). Also, noodles made from hearty, starchy vegetables can be stored in the refrigerator for a day or two before eating.

Per serving: Calories: 26; Total fat: 0g; Total carbs: 5g; Fiber: 2g; Sugar: 3g; Protein: 2g; Sodium: 133mg

1. Cut the ends off the zucchini. Make noodles with a spiralizer or mandoline, or simply run a vegetable or julienne peeler across the zucchini to create long, thin strips.

2. To reduce moisture, place the noodles in a colander and toss with sea salt. Let them sit for 30 minutes. Place the colander in a sink or over a large bowl to avoid a mess. Squeeze any excess moisture out with your hands and pat dry with a towel.

3. Zucchini noodles can be eaten raw, but cooking them will help keep them from getting too watery. To cook, place them in a single layer in a large sauté pan over medium-high heat and cook for 4 to 5 minutes. Depending on the size of the pan, this may need to be done in batches. Zucchini noodles are best when eaten right away.

CAULIFLOWER RICE

GLUTEN-FREE | LOW-CARB | NUT-FREE | SOY-FREE | OIL-FREE OPTION

SERVES 4 | PREP TIME: 5 minutes | COOK TIME: 10 minutes

Much like zucchini noodles, cauliflower rice started out as a popular dish in the raw food world before it hit the mainstream. You can buy bags of prepared cauliflower rice, but you never know how fresh they are, so I prefer to make it at home. It can be used in any dish that calls for cooked rice, such as stir-fries, my Garlicky Vegetable Fried Rice (see page 140), and my Buddha Bowls (see page 138). It can be eaten raw or cooked to take the bite out of it.

1 head cauliflower, cut into florets
1 teaspoon neutral-flavored oil (such as grapeseed or avocado)
Sea salt
Black pepper

Substitution tip: If you're feeling like you're going to turn into a cauliflower from eating so much of it, you can "rice" different vegetables. Broccoli and kohlrabi work well in this recipe, and even hearty vegetables like sweet potatoes, butternut squash, and beets can be used. Try using my Home-made Vegetable Stock (see page 20) or water in place of the neutral-flavored oil.

Per serving: Calories: 46; Total fat: 1g; Total carbs: 8g; Fiber: 4g; Sugar: 4g; Protein: 3g; Sodium: 55mg

1. If you're using a food processor: Coarsely chop the cauliflower into medium-size florets. Place them in the food processor and pulse until it resembles rice. If you're using a box grater: Cut the cauliflower into large chunks. Use the medium-size holes in your grater to grate the cauliflower.

2. Cauliflower rice can be eaten raw as is, or it can be cooked to soften it up. To cook it, heat the oil in a large sauté pan over medium-high heat. Add the cauliflower and cook, stirring frequently, for 5 to 10 minutes, or until it softens. Season with sea salt and black pepper.

CREAMY CAULIFLOWER SAUCE

GLUTEN-FREE | LOW-CARB | NUT-FREE | OIL-FREE | SOY-FREE

MAKES about 4 cups | PREP TIME: 10 minutes | COOK TIME: 15 minutes

Cauliflower is an amazing vegetable and, in recent years, it's become the vegan foodie's best friend. It can be minced to resemble rice, turned into a pizza crust, and blended into a deliciously creamy sauce. This sauce can be used in soups and sauces, on pasta, and even in my Creamed Kale (see page 104).

1 medium-size head cauliflower, chopped
  into medium-size florets (about
  5 or 6 cups)
3 garlic cloves
Water
½ teaspoon sea salt

Ingredient tip: Most grocery stores carry pre-chopped cauliflower, which cuts prep time down to almost nothing.

Per serving (1 cup): Calories: 39; Total fat: 0g; Total carbs: 8g; Fiber: 4g; Sugar: 4g; Protein: 3g; Sodium: 278mg

1. Place the cauliflower and garlic in a stockpot and fill it with enough water to cover the vegetables, plus about two inches.

2. Bring the water to a boil over medium-high heat. Reduce heat to medium-low and let the vegetables simmer for about 10 minutes, or until they are fork-tender.

3. Drain the cauliflower and garlic and save 2 cups of the drained water. Let the cauliflower and garlic cool slightly, and then place them in a high-speed blender or food processor along with the reserved cooking water and sea salt. Blend until smooth and creamy.

4. Pour the sauce in a medium-size saucepan and place it over medium-high heat. Bring the sauce to a boil. Reduce the heat to medium-low and let the sauce simmer for about 5 minutes, until it thickens slightly.

CHEESY VEGETABLE SAUCE

GLUTEN-FREE | LOW-CARB | NUT-FREE OPTION | OIL-FREE | SOY-FREE

MAKES about 5½ cups | PREP TIME: 10 minutes | COOK TIME: 20 minutes

Vegetables magically blend together with a few other ingredients to create a cheese-like sauce that will have even the pickiest eaters coming back for more. This sauce is perfect for making my Mac and "Cheese" with Broccoli (see page 133), and it's terrific on a baked potato or over roasted veggies.

2 medium-size carrots, chopped

2 cups chopped cauliflower

½ cup unsalted raw cashews

½ cup chopped roasted red pepper

½ cup nutritional yeast

1 tablespoon lemon juice

1 teaspoon Dijon mustard

1 teaspoon garlic powder

1 teaspoon onion powder

1 teaspoon sea salt

Ingredient tip: Nutritional yeast, affectionately known as "nooch" to many, may be difficult to find, but it's well worth the search; it's what gives this sauce its cheesy flavor. Some grocery stores keep it in the supplement aisle, while others may have it with the baking supplies.

Per serving (1/2 cup): Calories: 115; Total fat: 0g; Total carbs: 11g; Fiber: 4g; Sugar: 2g; Protein: 8g; Sodium: 185mg

1. Place the carrots, cauliflower, and cashews in a stockpot and fill it with enough water to cover the vegetables plus about two inches.

2. Bring the water to a boil over medium-high heat. Reduce the heat to medium-low and let the vegetables simmer for about 15 minutes, or until they are fork-tender.

3. Drain the vegetables and save 2 cups of the drained water. Let the vegetables cool slightly, and then place them in a high-speed blender or food processor. Add the roasted red pepper, nutritional yeast, lemon juice, mustard, garlic powder, onion powder, and sea salt. Add the reserved cooking water and blend until creamy.

4. Pour the sauce in a medium-size saucepan and place it over medium-high heat. Bring the sauce to a boil. Reduce the heat to medium-low and let the sauce simmer for about 5 minutes, until it thickens slightly.

TAHINI DRESSING

GLUTEN-FREE | LOW-CARB | NUT-FREE | OIL-FREE | SOY-FREE

MAKES about 1 cup | PREP TIME: 5 minutes

This is my go-to condiment, and I always have a jar of it in my refrigerator. I like to use it as a dressing on my salads as well as a dip for carrot sticks and celery. I've also been known to use it instead of mayonnaise on sandwiches and in coleslaw and potato salad. The thickness of different store-bought tahini brands can vary greatly, so you may need to add more water if your tahini is on the thick side. This dressing will thicken as it sits, so you might need to add a little more water if you're not using it right away.

½ cup tahini

¼ cup water, plus more if needed

3 tablespoons lemon juice

½ teaspoon garlic powder

¼ teaspoon sea salt

Combine tahini, water, lemon juice, garlic powder, and sea salt in a medium-size bowl and whisk until smooth and creamy. If the mixture is too thick, you can add more water, 1 tablespoon at a time, until it reaches the desired consistency. This dressing can be stored in the refrigerator for up to a week.

Speed it up: A blender can be used to mix up the dressing in seconds.

Per serving (2 tablespoons): Calories: 91; Total fat: 8g; Total carbs: 3g; Fiber: 1g; Sugar: 0g; Protein: 2g; Sodium: 77mg

SPICY PEANUT DRESSING

GLUTEN-FREE OPTION | LOW-CARB | OIL-FREE

MAKES about ¾ cup | PREP TIME: 5 minutes

I'm a real sucker for my Spicy Peanut Dressing. I love it on salads and noodles, in stir-fries, and even as a snack with carrot sticks. If you want to turn up the heat, add more crushed red pepper flakes. If spicy food isn't your thing, you can use less (or none) of it. When purchasing peanut butter, look for the natural type with no added oils or sugars. The ingredients should just be peanuts. If you're sensitive to gluten, use wheat-free tamari instead of soy sauce.

⅓ cup unsalted, natural creamy peanut butter

3 tablespoons water

2 tablespoons lime juice

2 tablespoons low-sodium soy sauce (or tamari)

2 teaspoons maple syrup (or agave)

½ teaspoon garlic powder

½ teaspoon ground ginger powder

½ teaspoon crushed red pepper flakes

In a medium bowl, mix together peanut butter, water, lime juice, soy sauce, maple syrup, garlic powder, ginger powder, and red pepper flakes with a fork or small whisk until smooth and creamy. If the mixture is too thick, add more water, 1 tablespoon at a time, until it reaches the desired consistency. This dressing can be stored in the refrigerator for up to a week.

Speed it up: You can use a blender to mix this dressing up in a few seconds.

Per serving (2 tablespoons): Calories: 213; Total fat: 16g; Total carbs: 8g; Fiber: 2g; Sugar: 3g; Protein: 8g; Sodium: 203mg

QUICK AND EASY TOMATO SAUCE

GLUTEN-FREE I LOW-CARB I NUT-FREE I SOY-FREE I OIL-FREE OPTION

MAKES about 4 cups I PREP TIME: 5 minutes I COOK TIME: 25 minutes

With hidden roasted red peppers, this tomato sauce is a sneaky way to get picky eaters to eat more veggies. When making tomato sauce at home, you can control the ingredients. If you'd like to add more fresh herbs, such as thyme or rosemary, or a little bit of crushed red pepper for heat, add them at the end with the basil, salt, and pepper.

1 (12-ounce) jar roasted red peppers

1 teaspoon neutral-flavored oil (such as grapeseed or avocado)

½ cup diced onion (about ¼ of an onion)

2 garlic cloves, minced

1 (28-ounce) can crushed tomatoes

2 tablespoons tomato paste

1 tablespoon dried basil (or 3 tablespoons minced fresh basil)

Sea salt

Black pepper

Slow it down: If you're not in a hurry, you can let the sauce simmer on medium-low for 45 minutes to 1 hour. The longer it simmers, the more flavorful it will be.

Substitution tip: Try using my Homemade Vegetable Stock (see page 20) or water in place of the neutral-flavored oil.

Per serving (1 cup): Calories: 126; Total fat: 1g; Total carbs: 25g; Fiber: 8g; Sugar: 16g; Protein: 6g; Sodium: 315mg

1. Drain and rinse the roasted red peppers. Purée them in a food processor or blender.

2. Heat the oil in a large saucepan over medium-high heat. Add the onion and cook for about 5 minutes, until they begin to brown.

3. Add the garlic and cook for about 1 minute more, until it begins to soften.

4. Add the crushed tomatoes, tomato paste, and puréed roasted red peppers to the saucepan. Stir to combine and lower the heat to medium-low. Let the sauce simmer uncovered for about 15 minutes, or until it thickens slightly.

5. Add the basil to the saucepan along with the sea salt and black pepper to taste.

6. Use immediately or place in an airtight container in the refrigerator or freezer. It will last for about 5 days in the refrigerator, or it can be frozen for several months.

BAKED TOFU

GLUTEN-FREE OPTION | LOW-CARB | NUT-FREE | OIL-FREE

SERVES 4 | PREP TIME: 10 minutes | COOK TIME: 30 minutes

Baking tofu makes it heartier and more flavorful. It can be used in salads, bowls, stir-fries, and served with dip as a snack or appetizer. Tofu tends to be watery, so if you're not going to bake it right away, wrap it in a towel and place it in the refrigerator for an hour or two. If you've got more time on your hands, you can marinate the tofu longer for a stronger flavor.

1 (14-ounce) block of firm tofu, drained, patted dry, and cut into 1-inch cubes

2 tablespoons low-sodium tamari (or soy sauce)

2 tablespoons rice vinegar (or apple cider vinegar)

½ teaspoon garlic powder

1 tablespoon cornstarch (or arrowroot)

Prep tip: To prepare your tofu to bake, drain off as much water as possible, then use a towel to blot off any excess water. If you'd like to use your baked tofu in a sandwich or wrap, slice it into rectangular slabs, about 1/4-inch thick. Slabs of tofu will only need to bake for 20 minutes, and they will need to be flipped after 10 minutes.

Per serving: Calories: 87; Total fat: 4g; Total carbs: 5g; Fiber: 1g; Sugar: 1g; Protein: 9g; Sodium: 225mg

1. Preheat your oven to 400°F and line a baking sheet with parchment paper.

2. Place the tofu in a medium-size bowl or shallow dish. Whisk together the tamari, rice vinegar, and garlic powder and pour it over the tofu. Toss the tofu to coat it well. Let it sit for about 5 minutes to absorb the liquid.

3. Sprinkle the cornstarch on the tofu and toss to coat.

4. Place the tofu pieces on the baking sheet and bake for 30 minutes, flipping the pieces after 15 minutes.

HEARTY VEGGIE CRUMBLES

GLUTEN-FREE OPTION | LOW-CARB | SOY-FREE | OIL-FREE OPTION

MAKES about 3 cups | PREP TIME: 10 minutes | COOK TIME: 10 minutes

Veggie crumbles resemble ground beef in both texture and appearance, and they can be used in a number of dishes. Mix them with taco seasoning for hearty tacos, add them to stews for a little oomph, or use them on pizzas. If you're allergic to nuts, raw sunflower seeds can be used. Soak the seeds in water for about two hours and then drain and rinse them before using.

3 cups cauliflower florets

4 ounces cremini mushrooms (or white button mushrooms)

½ cup walnuts

1 tablespoon low-sodium tamari (or soy sauce)

2 tablespoons tomato paste

1 teaspoon neutral-flavored oil (such as grapeseed or avocado)

Prep tip: If you don't have a food processor, chop the cauliflower, mushrooms, and walnuts into small bite-size pieces with a sharp knife.

Substitution tip: Try using my Homemade Vegetable Stock (see page 20) or water in place of the neutral-flavored oil.

Per serving (1/2 cup): Calories: 151; Total fat: 13g; Total carbs: 7g; Fiber: 3g; Sugar: 3g; Protein: 5g; Sodium: 122mg

1. Place the cauliflower florets in a food processor and pulse until they are ground into small pieces resembling rice. Place the cauliflower in a large bowl.

2. Place the mushrooms in the food processor and pulse until they are ground into small pieces, about 1/4-inch in size. Add them to the bowl with the cauliflower.

3. Place the walnuts in the food processor and pulse a few times until they resemble large crumbs. Don't overprocess, or they may turn into walnut butter. Add the walnuts to the bowl with the cauliflower and mushrooms.

4. Whisk the tamari and tomato paste together in a small bowl, and then pour it over the cauliflower mixture. Toss to coat.

5. Heat the oil in a large sauté pan over medium-high heat. Add the cauliflower mixture to the pan, and cook for about 10 minutes, stirring often, until the vegetables have softened.

Spinach-Mushroom Frittata, 42

CHAPTER THREE

BREAKFASTS

PIÑA COLADA GREEN SMOOTHIES

GLUTEN-FREE | NUT-FREE | OIL-FREE | SOY-FREE

SERVES 4 | PREP TIME: 5 minutes

There's really no better way to start the day than with a taste of the tropics. Baby spinach lends itself nicely to this smoothie and provides a significant amount of nutrients—including iron, magnesium, vitamins A, C, and K—without altering the drink's flavor. If you'd like to add a little protein to your smoothie, throw in a tablespoon or two of hempseeds.

2 bananas, peeled and sliced

2 cups frozen pineapple chunks

2 cups fresh baby spinach

1 (14-ounce) can light coconut milk

1 cup pineapple juice

½ cup ice (2 or 3 cubes)

Combine bananas, pineapple chunks, spinach, coconut milk, pineapple juice, and ice cubes and blend until smooth and creamy.

Prep tip: To speed things up, I like to put together smoothie bags. To do this, combine the dry ingredients in large freezer bags and pop them in the freezer at the beginning of the week. In the morning, just throw the contents of the bag into your blender along with the liquid, then blend and go! If your banana slices are frozen, you can skip the ice cubes.

Per serving: Calories: 200; Total fat: 5g; Total carbs: 38g; Fiber: 3g; Sugar: 25g; Protein: 2g; Sodium: 44mg

BASIC TOFU SCRAMBLE

GLUTEN-FREE | LOW-CARB | NUT-FREE | OIL-FREE OPTION

SERVES 4 | PREP TIME: 5 minutes, plus time to press the tofu | COOK TIME: 10 minutes

The tofu scramble is probably the quintessential vegan breakfast. It's incredibly versatile, too. You can sauté vegetables such as red pepper, onions, and mushrooms before adding the tofu to the pan. Baby spinach or arugula can be stirred in a minute or two before, removing the tofu scramble from the heat. This dish can be served on its own, paired with home fries and toast, or in my Breakfast Burritos (see page 41).

1 (14-ounce) block firm tofu, drained
  and pressed
1 teaspoon ground turmeric
½ teaspoon onion powder
½ teaspoon black pepper
½ teaspoon sea salt
1 teaspoon neutral-flavored oil (such as
  grapeseed or avocado)

Prep tip: This recipe uses water-packed firm tofu. To prepare it, drain off as much of the water as possible. Then, wrap it in a towel and place something heavy on top of it, such as a cast-iron skillet or a cutting board with a few cans of beans on top. Let it sit for 30 to 60 minutes.

Substitution tip: Try using my Homemade Vegetable Stock (see page 20) or water in place of the neutral-flavored oil.

Per serving: Calories: 82; Total fat: 5g; Total carbs: 2g; Fiber: 1g; Sugar: 1g; Protein: 8g; Sodium: 246mg

1. Place the tofu in a large bowl and use a large fork or potato masher to crumble it into small, bite-size pieces. Add the turmeric, onion powder, black pepper, and sea salt to the tofu and toss to coat.

2. Heat the oil in a large sauté pan or cast-iron pan over medium-high heat. Add the tofu and cook, stirring frequently, for 8 to 10 minutes, or until it begins to brown.

BLUEBERRY PIE OVERNIGHT OATS

GLUTEN-FREE | OIL-FREE | SOY-FREE OPTION

SERVES 2 | PREP TIME: 5 minutes, plus 5 hours refrigerator time

Breakfast doesn't get any easier than overnight oats. You simply throw the ingredients together in a jar, give it a good shake, pop it in the refrigerator, and your morning meal is ready when you wake up. If you're sensitive to gluten, make sure your rolled oats are certified gluten-free. Oats are gluten-free by nature, but they can pick up minute traces of it on cross-contaminated processing equipment.

1½ cups plain, unsweetened nondairy milk
  (such as soy or almond)
1 cup rolled oats
2 tablespoons maple syrup
1 teaspoon vanilla extract
1 teaspoon ground cinnamon
2 cups fresh blueberries
¼ cup almonds, coarsely chopped

1. Place the nondairy milk, oats, maple syrup, vanilla extract, and cinnamon in a large jar or container with a lid. Shake until everything is mixed together. Top with the blueberries and almonds. Place in your refrigerator for at least 5 hours.

2. Just before serving, stir to mix the blueberries and almonds into the oatmeal.

Substitution tip: Not in the mood for blueberries? Just about any berry will work in this recipe. Diced apples or pears are delicious, too.

Per serving: Calories: 438; Total fat: 15g; Total carbs: 67g; Fiber: 12g; Sugar: 28g; Protein: 11g; Sodium: 265mg

CARROT CAKE OATMEAL

GLUTEN-FREE | NUT-FREE OPTION | OIL-FREE | SOY-FREE OPTION

SERVES 4 | PREP TIME: 5 minutes | COOK TIME: 15 minutes

I'm not a fan of mushy foods, and cooked oats always remind me of the lumpy paste I used in art class. Because it's full of nutrients—including fiber, magnesium, selenium, and iron—I've looked for ways to make it more palatable. One way is to include dried fruit and nuts to add texture. In this recipe, I've added grated carrots, making it seem more like dessert than a healthy breakfast.

2 cups water

2 cups nondairy milk, such as soy or almond

2 cups rolled oats

2 medium-size carrots, grated or shredded

1 tablespoon maple syrup

1 teaspoon cinnamon

1 teaspoon vanilla extract

¼ cup raisins

¼ cup chopped walnuts or pecans

1. Heat the water, nondairy milk, and rolled oats in a medium-size saucepan over medium-high heat. Bring to a boil, and then reduce to medium heat.

2. Stir in the carrots, maple syrup, cinnamon, vanilla extract, raisins, and walnuts. Cook for 5 to 10 more minutes, or until oatmeal has reached the desired consistency.

Slow it down: If you have the time, this recipe can be made in a slow cooker, so a hot breakfast will be waiting for you when you wake up in the morning. Place the water, nondairy milk, carrots, maple syrup, cinnamon, and vanilla extract in your slow cooker and cook on low for 8 hours. Stir the raisins and walnuts into the oatmeal right before serving. Slow cooker oatmeal is creamier than stovetop oats.

Per serving: Calories: 263; Total fat: 8g; Total carbs: 43g; Fiber: 6g; Sugar: 11g; Protein: 7g; Sodium: 25mg

CHERRY AND ALMOND BAKED GRANOLA

GLUTEN-FREE | OIL-FREE | SOY-FREE

MAKES about 5 cups | PREP TIME: 10 minutes | COOK TIME: 25 minutes

One of my go-to breakfast dishes for busy weekdays is nondairy yogurt parfaits layered with fresh fruit and baked granola. Most store-bought granola is loaded with oil, so I make my own using nut butters. In addition to layering it into parfaits, this granola can be enjoyed in a bowl with fresh fruit and nondairy milk. It's a terrific snack, too.

½ cup maple syrup

¼ cup natural almond butter

1 teaspoon vanilla extract

1 teaspoon cinnamon

½ teaspoon sea salt

1½ cups rolled oats

½ cup raw almonds, coarsely chopped

1 cup dried cherries

Substitution tip: I love the combination of cherries and almonds, but you can use any combination of nuts, dried fruit, and nut butter that you like.

Per serving (1/2 cup): Calories: 215; Total fat: 7g; Total carbs: 35g; Fiber: 8g; Sugar: 21g; Protein: 4g; Sodium: 97mg

1. Preheat oven to 325°F and line baking sheet with parchment paper.

2. In a medium bowl, whisk together maple syrup, almond butter, vanilla, cinnamon, and sea salt.

3. In a large bowl, combine the rolled oats and almonds. Add the maple syrup mixture to the bowl and stir to coat well.

4. Spread the mixture out evenly onto your prepared baking sheet. Bake for 20 to 25 minutes, stirring the mixture at the 10-minute mark. The granola is done when the oats are golden brown and the almonds look toasted.

5. Remove the granola from the oven and mix in the dried cherries. The granola will be soft, but it will crisp as it cools. Allow it to cool completely before eating or storing.

CRANBERRY AND PECAN BREAKFAST BARS

GLUTEN-FREE | LOW-CARB | OIL-FREE | SOY-FREE

MAKES 12 bars | PREP TIME: 10 minutes, plus 2 hours refrigerator time

These grab-and-go bars are perfect for busy mornings when there's absolutely no time to cook, and they make a great midmorning pick-me-up, too. I've used cranberries and pecans for a fall feel, but you can use any combination of nuts, seeds, nut butter, and dried fruits that you'd like. To make these bars nut-free, use sun butter made from sunflower seeds.

1 cup unsalted, natural almond butter

½ cup maple syrup

1 teaspoon cinnamon

2 cups rolled oats

½ cup dried cranberries

⅓ cup pumpkin seeds

⅓ cup toasted pecans

Make-ahead tip: These bars can be made ahead of time and stored in the freezer for up to 6 months. Wrap each individually in foil or freezer wrap and place them in the freezer. Prior to eating, defrost the bars at room temperature for about 15 minutes.

Per serving: Calories: 269; Total fat: 16g; Total carbs: 29g; Fiber: 5g; Sugar: 14g; Protein: 6g; Sodium: 6mg

1. Line an 8-by-8-inch baking dish with parchment paper.

2. In a medium bowl, stir together the almond butter, maple syrup, and cinnamon until well combined.

3. In a large bowl, stir together the rolled oats, dried cranberries, pumpkin seeds, and pecans until well combined. Pour the almond butter and maple syrup mixture into the bowl and stir to coat everything well. The mixture will be thick, so you may need to use your hands.

4. Transfer the mixture to the prepared dish and spread into an even layer. Use a spatula or wooden spoon to flatten and smooth the top.

5. Refrigerate for 1 to 2 hours, or until the mixture is firm. Remove the slab from the dish, place it on a cutting board, and cut it into 12 bars.

MORNING MUFFINS

LOW-CARB | NUT-FREE OPTION | OIL-FREE | SOY-FREE OPTION

MAKES **12** | PREP TIME: **10 minutes** | COOK TIME: **20 minutes**

Positioning the oven rack to the upper third of the oven to bake muffins is a trick I learned from Fran Costigan, the queen of vegan baking, and it's the key to nicely domed muffin tops. I start this recipe by clabbering nondairy milk with apple cider vinegar. Clabbering thickens and curdles the milk, which helps the muffins rise. It works best with almond or soy milk, but it doesn't always work with other nondairy milks.

½ cup plain, unsweetened almond milk (or soy milk)

1 tablespoon apple cider vinegar

1½ cups whole-wheat flour

1 teaspoon baking soda

1 teaspoon baking powder

½ teaspoon sea salt

1 teaspoon ground cinnamon

½ cup maple syrup

½ cup unsweetened applesauce

1 teaspoon vanilla extract

1 cup grated or shredded zucchini (about 1 small zucchini)

1 cup grated or shredded carrots (about 2 medium carrots)

¼ cup chopped pistachios

1. Position a rack in the upper third of the oven and preheat the oven to 350°F. Line a muffin pan with paper liners.

2. Mix the almond milk and apple cider vinegar together and set aside for 5 to 10 minutes.

3. In a large bowl, whisk together the flour, baking soda, baking powder, sea salt, and cinnamon.

4. In a medium bowl, whisk together the maple syrup, applesauce, vanilla extract, and almond milk mixture.

5. Pour the wet mixture into the dry mixture and mix until there are no visible lumps of flour. Do not overmix. The batter will be thick.

6. Carefully fold in the zucchini, carrots, and pistachios.

7. Divide the batter among the muffin cups, filling them three-quarters of the way full.

8. Bake for 17 to 20 minutes, until the muffins are golden brown around the edges and a toothpick inserted in the center comes out clean.

Make-ahead tip: These muffins can be made in advance and frozen in an airtight container for up to two months. Prior to eating, remove them from the freezer, take them out of the container, and leave them at room temperature for about 1 hour.

Per serving: Calories: 115; Total fat: 1g; Total carbs: 25g; Fiber: 1g; Sugar: 10g; Protein: 2g; Sodium: 203mg

APPLE-CINNAMON WHOLE-WHEAT PANCAKES

GLUTEN-FREE OPTION | NUT-FREE OPTION | SOY-FREE OPTION

SERVES 4 | PREP TIME: 10 minutes | COOK TIME: 15 minutes

These deliciously fluffy pancakes are loaded with apple and cinnamon goodness. Most people drown their pancakes with sugary syrup, but I think these are sweet enough as they are. I like to toss diced apple pieces with applesauce for my pancake topping. Any type of apple will work in this recipe, but I like to use Gala, Golden Delicious, or Honeycrisp.

1½ cups whole-wheat or gluten-free flour

1 tablespoon baking powder

1 teaspoon cinnamon

¼ teaspoon sea salt

1½ cups nondairy milk (such as soy or almond)

¼ cup unsweetened applesauce

2 tablespoons maple syrup

1 large apple, finely chopped

Neutral-flavored oil (such as grapeseed or avocado)

Make-ahead tip: Did you know that pancakes can be frozen? Just place a piece of wax paper or freezer paper between each one and store them in an airtight container in the freezer for up to 2 months. To heat them up, microwave them on high for 1½ minutes, or cook them on a baking sheet in the oven for 8 to 10 minutes.

Per serving: Calories: 289; Total fat: 5g; Total carbs: 55g; Fiber: 4g; Sugar: 13g; Protein: 6g; Sodium: 198mg

1. In a large bowl, whisk together the flour, baking powder, cinnamon, and sea salt.

2. In a small bowl, whisk together the nondairy milk, applesauce, and maple syrup. Pour the wet mixture into the dry and stir until they are just combined. Don't overmix the batter. Gently fold in the apple.

3. Lightly oil a large griddle or cast-iron pan over medium-high heat. When the pan is hot, spoon ½ cup of the batter onto the griddle and cook for 2 or 3 minutes, until small bubbles appear on the top and the edges look dry. Flip and cook for 1 to 2 minutes on the other side. Repeat with the remaining batter. Cover the pancakes so they stay hot while the rest are cooking.

BREAKFAST BURRITOS

GLUTEN-FREE OPTION | OIL-FREE OPTION

SERVES 4 | PREP TIME: 10 minutes | COOK TIME: 15 minutes

Have you noticed that wrapping food in a tortilla makes it even more delicious? In these breakfast burritos, I've combined my Basic Tofu Scramble with bell peppers and spinach in a big tortilla. Feel free to add other veggies if you like, such as mushrooms and zucchini, as well as sliced avocado.

1 teaspoon neutral-flavored oil (such as grapeseed or avocado)

½ small onion, chopped

2 garlic cloves, minced

1 red bell pepper, chopped

2 cups spinach, packed

Basic Tofu Scramble (see page 33)

¼ cup Cheesy Vegetable Sauce (see page 24)

4 large (10- to 12-inch) whole-wheat (or gluten-free) tortillas, warmed

Make-ahead tip: These burritos can be made ahead of time and frozen for those busy mornings when there's no time to cook. Just wrap each burrito tightly in foil and pop it in the freezer. When you're ready to eat, remove the foil and defrost them in a 350°F oven for 15 minutes or a microwave for 2 to 3 minutes.

Substitution tip: Try using my Homemade Vegetable Stock (see page 20) or water in place of the neutral-flavored oil.

Calories: 329; Total fat: 12g; Total carbs: 42g; Fiber: 4g; Sugar: 4g; Protein: 15g; Sodium: 446mg

1. Heat the oil in a large sauté pan or cast-iron pan over medium-high heat. Add the onion and cook for about 5 minutes, until it begins to brown. Add the garlic and bell pepper, and cook, stirring often, for about 5 more minutes, until they begin to soften. Add the spinach and cook for 1 to 2 minutes, until it wilts.

2. Spoon the Basic Tofu Scramble down the center of each tortilla. Top each with the cooked vegetables and a drizzle of Cheesy Vegetable Sauce. Roll the tortilla, tucking in the sides as you go.

SPINACH-MUSHROOM FRITTATA

GLUTEN-FREE | LOW-CARB | NUT-FREE OPTION | OIL-FREE OPTION

SERVES 4 | PREP TIME: 10 minutes, plus time to press the tofu | COOK TIME: 50 minutes

Brunch is my favorite meal, and I take it very seriously. I usually make a big brunch on Sundays with fresh fruit, whole grain toast, and a frittata like this one. I love the flavor combination of spinach and mushrooms, but if it isn't your thing, you can use almost any type of vegetable and leafy green. Red pepper and arugula would be great, as would zucchini and baby kale.

1 teaspoon neutral-flavored oil (such as grapeseed or avocado)

8 ounces cremini mushrooms (or white button mushrooms), coarsely chopped

2 garlic cloves, minced

1 (14-ounce) block of extra-firm tofu, drained and pressed (see tip on page 28)

3 tablespoons nutritional yeast

3 tablespoons plain, unsweetened nondairy milk (such as soy or almond)

2 tablespoons lemon juice

1 tablespoon cornstarch (or arrowroot)

½ teaspoon dried basil

½ teaspoon dried thyme

½ teaspoon turmeric

½ teaspoon sea salt

¼ teaspoon black pepper

5 ounces baby spinach

1. Preheat your oven to 375°F and lightly oil an 8-inch pie pan.

2. Heat the oil in a large sauté pan or cast-iron pan over medium-high heat. Add the mushrooms and garlic, and cook, stirring occasionally, until they begin to brown. Remove the pan from heat.

3. Place the tofu, nutritional yeast, nondairy milk, lemon juice, cornstarch, basil, thyme, turmeric, sea salt, and black pepper into a food processor and process until smooth.

4. Add the spinach and mushroom mixture to a food processor and pulse two or three times to incorporate. If you don't have a food processor, coarsely chop the spinach. Mash the tofu mixture together with a potato masher or large fork until all the large lumps are gone. Fold the mushrooms and spinach into the mixture.

5. Pour the tofu mixture into the prepared pie pan and smooth it with a spatula or wooden spoon. Bake for 40 to 45 minutes, or until the frittata is golden brown. Let the frittata sit for 10 to 15 minutes to firm up a little before slicing.

Make-ahead tip: If you want to sleep in on Sunday morning, you can cook the mushrooms and make the tofu mixture ahead of time and place them in the refrigerator overnight. In the morning, just pop it into a pan and bake it. Breakfast is served!

Substitution tip: Try using my Homemade Vegetable Stock (see page 20) or water in place of the neutral-flavored oil.

Per serving: Calories: 223; Total fat: 10g; Total carbs: 14g; Fiber: 6g; Sugar: 2g; Protein: 24g; Sodium: 287mg

Gado Gado, 60

CHAPTER FOUR

SALADS

GREEN GODDESS SALAD

GLUTEN-FREE | LOW-CARB | NUT-FREE | OIL FREE

SERVES 4 | PREP TIME: 15 minutes | COOK TIME: 3 minutes

The dressing for Green Goddess Salad is usually made with mayonnaise, anchovies, and fresh herbs such as tarragon and parsley. In my vegan version, I've used an avocado instead of oily mayo, and salty capers take the place of anchovies. I've omitted the tarragon simply because I don't like it—it's too reminiscent of licorice for my taste. I've included my favorite green vegetables in this salad, and I've blanched the asparagus to soften it. Asparagus can be eaten uncooked, but it can be a little tough. If asparagus isn't in season, try using broccoli.

FOR THE SALAD:

1 pound asparagus, tough ends removed

5 ounces spring mix

1 medium cucumber, chopped

1 cup edamame, shelled

1 cup pea shoots, broccoli sprouts, clover sprouts, or alfalfa sprouts

FOR THE DRESSING:

1 large avocado, peeled, pitted, and sliced

½ cup plain, unsweetened nondairy milk (such as soy or almond), plus more if needed

2 tablespoons lemon juice

2 teaspoons Dijon mustard

1 teaspoon capers, drained

1 garlic clove, minced

¼ cup chopped parsley

1 tablespoon chopped chives

1. Prepare a large bowl with ice water and bring a large pot of salted water to a boil. Add the asparagus to the boiling water and cook for about 3 minutes, or until it's bright green. Remove the asparagus stalks from the pot with tongs or a skimmer, and immediately transfer them to the ice water bowl. Let them sit in the ice water for a minute. Remove the asparagus stalks from the water, place them on a cutting board, and pat them dry with a towel. Chop them into bite-size pieces.

2. In a large bowl, toss together the spring mix, asparagus, cucumber, and edamame.

3. To make the dressing: Combine avocado, nondairy milk, lemon juice, mustard, capers, garlic, parsley, and chives in a food processor or blender until smooth and creamy. Add more nondairy milk, if needed.

4. Pour the dressing onto the salad and toss to coat the salad. Top with the pea shoots.

Ingredient tip: Edamame can sometimes be found shelled in packages in the produce department of grocery stores. If your grocery store has a fresh sushi counter, chances are that they'll have steamed edamame in their pods. Bags of the frozen variety can be found in the freezer section of the store. If you're using frozen edamame, defrost it before adding it to the salad.

Per serving: Calories: 222; Total fat: 12g; Total carbs: 21g; Fiber: 10g; Sugar: 4g; Protein: 14g; Sodium: 103mg

WHITE BEAN COBB SALAD

GLUTEN-FREE OPTION | NUT-FREE

SERVES 4 | PREP TIME: 15 minutes

The Cobb Salad was invented by Robert Cobb in the 1930s. Traditionally, it's made with a mix of chopped greens, tomato, bacon, chicken, hardboiled eggs, avocado, cheese, chives, and red wine vinaigrette. It's not even close to being vegan, but it's easily adaptable. I've used beans and my Baked Tofu for protein in this recipe, and I added corn for color. Cobb salads are typically served with the greens as a base on a large platter, and the rest of the ingredients are arranged in colorful rows on top of them.

FOR THE SALAD:

6 cups chopped romaine lettuce (about 1 large head)

2 cups chopped watercress

16 ounces Baked Tofu (see page 28), or store-bought baked tofu, cut into cubes

1 pint cherry (or grape) tomatoes, sliced in half

1 avocado, chopped

1 cup cooked cannellini beans (or great northern beans)

1 cup corn kernels, fresh or frozen and thawed

FOR THE DRESSING:

¼ cup red wine vinegar

¼ cup extra-virgin olive oil

1 tablespoon Dijon mustard

1 teaspoon maple syrup

2 tablespoons chopped chives

1. To make the salad: In a large bowl, toss together the romaine and watercress. Arrange the greens on a large plate or platter. Arrange the tofu, tomatoes, avocado, beans, and corn in rows over the greens.

2. To make the dressing: In a small bowl, whisk together vinegar, olive oil, mustard, maple syrup, and chives.

3. Drizzle the dressing over the salad and serve.

Substitution tip: Tempeh bacon would be a delicious substitute for baked tofu. It can usually be found in the same grocer area as tofu. Chickpeas or kidney beans can be substituted for the cannellini or great northern beans. If watercress can't be found, you can use Bibb or butter lettuce in its place.

Per serving: Calories: 385; Total fat: 25g; Total carbs: 30g; Fiber: 9g; Sugar: 7g; Protein: 17g; Sodium: 83mg

SPINACH AND STRAWBERRY SALAD

GLUTEN-FREE | LOW-CARB | SOY-FREE

SERVES 4 | PREP TIME: **15 minutes**

This type of salad is usually made with feta cheese, but I've used a diced avocado in its place. This salad is perfect for spring and summer, but it can easily be altered for cool weather months by using a sliced pear in place of the strawberries and chopped pecans or walnuts in place of the almonds.

FOR THE SALAD:

5 ounces baby spinach
1 pint strawberries, hulled and quartered
1 large avocado, peeled, pitted, and diced
¼ cup almonds, coarsely chopped

FOR THE DRESSING:

¼ cup balsamic vinegar
2 tablespoons extra-virgin olive oil
1 tablespoon maple syrup
1½ tablespoons poppy seeds
1 teaspoon Dijon mustard

1. To make the salad: In a large bowl, toss together the spinach, strawberries, and avocado.

2. To make the dressing: In a small bowl, whisk together the vinegar, olive oil, maple syrup, poppy seeds, and mustard.

3. Pour the dressing over the salad and toss to combine everything. Top the salad with the chopped almonds.

Substitution tip: Even though this is a *spinach* salad, arugula or baby kale can be used as the salad's base.

Per serving: Calories: 238; Total fat: 19g; Total carbs: 18g; Fiber: 7g; Sugar: 8g; Protein: 4g; Sodium: 48mg

ARUGULA AND APPLE SALAD

GLUTEN-FREE | OIL-FREE | SOY-FREE

SERVES 4 | PREP TIME: **15 minutes**

This salad has a fall flair to it, but it can easily be adapted for summer or spring. Instead of an apple, you can use a cup of fresh berries. Almonds or pistachios can be used instead of pecans, sunflower seeds can be used instead of pumpkin seeds, and dried cherries can be used in the place of dried cranberries. The maple-mustard dressing is one of my favorites. I suggest doubling it and keeping a batch in the refrigerator for future salads. It's a great dip for carrot sticks, too.

FOR THE SALAD:

5 ounces arugula

2 carrots, shredded or grated

1 apple, chopped

¼ cup toasted pecans, chopped

¼ cup pumpkin seeds

¼ cup unsweetened dried cranberries

FOR THE DRESSING:

2 tablespoons tahini

2 tablespoons water, plus more if needed

1 tablespoon apple cider vinegar

1 tablespoon maple syrup

1 teaspoon Dijon mustard

½ teaspoon garlic powder

¼ teaspoon sea salt

1. To make the salad: In a large bowl, toss together the arugula, carrots, and apple.

2. To make the dressing: In a small bowl, whisk together the tahini, water, vinegar, maple syrup, mustard, garlic powder, and sea salt. If the mixture is too thick, add more water, 1 teaspoon at a time.

3. Pour the dressing over the salad and toss to combine everything. Top the salad with the pecans, pumpkin seeds, and cranberries.

Ingredient tip: The process of dehydrating dried fruits causes their sugars to concentrate. Some manufacturers add sugar to dried fruit, especially cranberries, because of their tartness. Be sure to read the ingredients to make certain that your dried fruit contains only dried fruit and no added sugar.

Per serving: Calories: 249; Total fat: 13g; Total carbs: 30g; Fiber: 6g; Sugar: 17g; Protein: 6g; Sodium: 173mg

RAINBOW KALE SALAD

GLUTEN-FREE OPTION | LOW-CARB | NUT-FREE | OIL-FREE

SERVES 4 | PREP TIME: **15 minutes**

Raw kale can be a little tough, but massaging it makes it easier to eat. Lemon juice or vinegar can soften the leaves, and they can also help release some of kale's sweetness, balancing out the bitter taste it sometimes has in its raw state. Simply pour on a little dressing and gently knead the kale, similar to the way you'd knead dough. It only needs to be massaged for three or four minutes—overdoing it will leave your salad too wilted.

FOR THE DRESSING:

¼ cup tahini
¼ cup apple cider vinegar
2 tablespoons water, plus more if needed
1 medium carrot
1 tablespoon low-sodium tamari (or soy sauce)
1 tablespoon maple syrup
1 (1-inch) piece ginger, peeled and coarsely chopped

FOR THE SALAD:

6 cups chopped curly kale, tough stems removed
2 cups thinly sliced red cabbage
2 carrots, grated or shredded
1 medium beet, peeled and grated
3 medium radishes, thinly sliced

1. To make the dressing: Combine tahini, vinegar, water, carrot, tamari, maple syrup, and ginger in a food processor or blender until smooth and creamy. If the mixture is too thick, add more water, 1 teaspoon at a time.

2. To make the salad: Place the kale in a large bowl and pour half of the dressing over it. With clean hands, gently massage the dressing into the kale until the leaves are completely coated and have softened slightly.

CONTINUED

3. Add the cabbage, carrots, beet, and radishes to the bowl, and toss to combine. Drizzle the rest of the dressing on top of the salad.

Prep tip: If your food processor has a grating attachment, it can grate your carrots and beet in seconds. Some stores carry pre-grated veggies in their produce departments, making prep even easier.

Per serving: Calories: 198; Total fat: 8g; Total carbs: 27g; Fiber: 6g; Sugar: 9g; Protein: 7g; Sodium: 270mg

TACO SALAD

GLUTEN-FREE | LOW-CARB | NUT-FREE | OIL-FREE | SOY-FREE

SERVES 4 | PREP TIME: **15 minutes**

I love a good vegan taco! If I have taco leftovers from dinner, I like to pile them into a big salad for lunch the next day. In this recipe, I've skipped the taco-cooking step and gone straight for the salad. I've used lettuce, tomato, corn, beans, and avocado in this recipe, but feel free to add your favorite taco toppings. A little salsa and a few jalapeño slices would make great additions.

FOR THE SALAD:

1 (15-ounce) can black beans, drained
  and rinsed
1 teaspoon lime juice
1½ teaspoons chili powder
½ teaspoon onion powder
½ teaspoon garlic powder
½ teaspoon sea salt
6 cups chopped romaine lettuce
1 cup corn kernels, fresh or frozen
  and thawed
1 tomato, diced
1 large avocado, peeled, pitted,
  and chopped

FOR THE DRESSING:

1 large avocado, peeled, pitted, and sliced
¼ cup lime juice
2 tablespoons water, plus more if needed
1 garlic clove, minced
¼ teaspoon red pepper flakes
¼ teaspoon sea salt

1. Place the black beans in a medium bowl. Add the lime juice, chili powder, onion powder, garlic powder, and sea salt. Toss well to coat the black beans.

2. To make the dressing: Combine the avocado, lime juice, water, garlic, red pepper flakes, and sea salt in a food processor or blender until smooth and creamy. If the mixture is too thick, add more water, 1 teaspoon at a time.

3. In a large bowl, toss together the romaine lettuce, corn, tomato, avocado, and black beans. Pour the dressing over the salad and toss to combine everything.

Substitution tip: Pinto or kidney beans can be used instead of black beans. My Hearty Veggie Crumbles (see page 29) can be used as well.

Per serving: Calories: 230; Total fat: 14g; Total carbs: 24g; Fiber: 12g; Sugar: 5g; Protein: 7g; Sodium: 192mg

CHICKPEA NIÇOISE SALAD

GLUTEN-FREE | NUT-FREE | SOY-FREE

SERVES 4 | PREP TIME: 15 minutes | COOK TIME: 5 minutes

The niçoise salad originated in Nice, France. It's traditionally made with tomatoes, hardboiled eggs, niçoise olives, anchovies, and olive oil, although tuna, cooked potatoes, and green beans are commonly added. I've read that purists will defend the traditional version and shun any deviations. I'm guessing they wouldn't be too happy with this vegan version, but I certainly like it! This salad can be served tossed or composed in rows, similar to the arrangement of a typical Cobb salad. I've composed it in rows here, but feel free to toss everything together.

FOR THE SALAD:

8 ounces small new potatoes, cut in half

½ pound green beans, trimmed

1 (15-ounce) can chickpeas, rinsed and drained

6 cups chopped Boston lettuce (or green leaf lettuce)

1 pint grape (or cherry) tomatoes, sliced in half

½ cup niçoise (or kalamata) olives, pitted

FOR THE DRESSING:

¼ cup white wine vinegar

2 tablespoons extra-virgin olive oil

1 tablespoon Dijon mustard

1 tablespoon capers, drained and rinsed

½ teaspoon dried basil

½ teaspoon dried oregano

1. Prepare a large bowl with ice water and bring a large pot of salted water to a boil. Add the potatoes to the boiling water and cook for 3 minutes.

2. Add the green beans to the pot with the potatoes and continue to cook for 2 more minutes. The potatoes should be fork-tender, and the green beans should be bright green.

3. Remove the vegetables from the pot with a skimmer or slotted spoon and immediately transfer them to the ice water bowl. Let them sit in the ice water for a minute. Drain the vegetables, place them on a plate or cutting board, and pat them dry with a towel.

4. To make the dressing, in a small bowl, whisk together the vinegar, olive oil, mustard, capers, basil, and oregano.

5. In another small bowl, gently mash the chickpeas with a fork or potato masher.

6. Assemble the lettuce on a large platter. Arrange the potatoes, green beans, mashed chickpeas, tomatoes, and olives in rows on top of the lettuce. Drizzle the dressing onto the salad.

Make-ahead tip: The potatoes and green beans can be prepared ahead of time and stored in the refrigerator until you're ready to make the salad.

Per serving: Calories: 290; Total fat: 11g; Total carbs: 43g; Fiber: 10g; Sugar: 13g; Protein: 9g; Sodium: 272mg

CHICKPEA GYRO SALAD

GLUTEN-FREE | LOW-CARB | NUT-FREE | OIL-FREE | SOY-FREE

SERVES 4 | PREP TIME: **15 minutes**

A gyro is a Greek sandwich made from meat cooked on a large, vertical rotisserie. It's usually wrapped in a pita or flatbread and served with a yogurt sauce. I've never actually had one because I was vegetarian when I first learned they existed, but I have had vegan versions and I've loved them. In this salad, I've tossed chickpeas in spices similar to those used to cook gyros, and I've combined them with fresh vegetables and my Tahini Dressing.

1 (15-ounce) can chickpeas, drained
   and rinsed

1 teaspoon dried oregano

1 teaspoon dried thyme

½ teaspoon cumin

½ teaspoon turmeric

¼ teaspoon black pepper

6 cups chopped romaine lettuce (about
   1 large head)

½ red onion, thinly sliced

1 red bell pepper, chopped

1 tomato, diced

½ cup Tahini Dressing (see page 25)

1. Place the chickpeas in a medium bowl and add the oregano, thyme, cumin, turmeric, and black pepper. Toss the chickpeas in the spices to coat.

2. In a large bowl, toss together the romaine lettuce, bell pepper, and tomato. Pour the dressing over the salad and toss to combine everything. Top with the spiced chickpeas.

Ingredient tip: Save that chickpea liquid! It's known as "aquafaba," and it's pretty magical. It can be whipped up like eggs to make meringues, and it can sometimes be used as an egg-replacer in baking. I like to use it in place of oil when roasting and baking.

Per serving: Calories: 225; Total fat: 10g; Total carbs: 27g; Fiber: 7g; Sugar: 6g; Protein: 9g; Sodium: 89mg

FATTOUSH SALAD

GLUTEN-FREE | NUT-FREE | SOY-FREE

SERVES 4 | PREP TIME: 15 minutes | COOK TIME: 30 minutes

I love Middle Eastern restaurants because they tend to be veg-friendly. They usually have hummus, falafel, and tabbouleh, all of which are traditionally vegan. I first tried a fattoush salad about 15 years ago in a local Middle Eastern restaurant and I was hooked. They are typically made with toasted or fried pieces of flatbread but in this version, I've used roasted chickpeas. There's no need to rinse the chickpeas after you drain them. The liquid from the can (aka aquafaba) will help the chickpeas crisp up while roasting.

FOR THE SALAD:

1 (15-ounce) can chickpeas, drained

½ teaspoon sea salt

½ teaspoon black pepper

6 cups chopped romaine lettuce (about
    1 large head)

½ red onion, thinly sliced

1 small cucumber, chopped

1 pint grape (or cherry) tomatoes,
    sliced in half

½ cup chopped flat leaf parsley

FOR THE DRESSING:

2 tablespoons olive oil

2 tablespoons lemon juice

2 tablespoons red wine vinegar

2 teaspoons sumac

1 garlic clove, minced

1. Preheat your oven to 425°F and line a baking sheet with parchment paper.

2. Place the chickpeas in a medium bowl and sprinkle on the sea salt and black pepper. Toss to coat them well.

3. Transfer the chickpeas to the prepared baking sheet and bake them for 30 minutes, tossing them about halfway through to make sure they roast evenly. Let cool for 10 minutes.

4. While the chickpeas are roasting, place the romaine lettuce, onion, tomatoes, cucumber, and parsley in a large bowl and toss to mix.

CONTINUED

5. In a small bowl, whisk together the olive oil, lemon juice, vinegar, sumac, and garlic. Pour the dressing over the salad and toss to combine. Top with the roasted chickpeas.

Substitution tip: Sumac is a common spice in Middle Eastern cooking, and it's traditionally used in fattoush salads. It has a tart, lemony flavor. If your local grocery store doesn't carry it, use 2 teaspoons of paprika in its place and add 1/2 teaspoon of lemon zest to the dressing.

Per serving: Calories: 228; Total fat: 9g; Total carbs: 32g; Fiber: 6g; Sugar: 13g; Protein: 7g; Sodium: 252mg

PEANUTTY THAI SALAD

GLUTEN-FREE OPTION | LOW-CARB | OIL-FREE

SERVES 4 | PREP TIME: 15 minutes

I love spicy peanut sauce so much that sometimes I'll plan my meals around it. This chopped, Thai-style salad is one of my favorite peanut sauce vehicles. I've used my favorite ingredients in this recipe, but you can adapt it to suit whatever you have on hand. Sliced cucumbers, diced tomatoes, and even chopped mangos would all make excellent additions.

6 cups chopped Napa cabbage

1 red bell pepper, chopped

2 medium-size carrots, chopped

1 cup edamame, shelled

1 cup mung bean sprouts

½ cup chopped cilantro

½ cup Spicy Peanut Dressing (see page 26), or store-bought spicy peanut dressing

¼ cup unsalted, roasted peanuts, chopped

In a large bowl, toss together the cabbage, bell pepper, carrots, edamame, mung bean sprouts, and cilantro. Pour the dressing on the salad and toss to combine. Top with the chopped peanuts.

Substitution tip: If Napa cabbage isn't available, you can use green cabbage or romaine lettuce in its place.

Per serving: Calories: 409; Total fat: 25g; Total carbs: 27g; Fiber: 8g; Sugar: 8g; Protein: 23g; Sodium: 379mg

GADO GADO

GLUTEN-FREE OPTION | LOW-CARB | OIL-FREE

SERVEs 4 | PREP TIME: **15 minutes** | COOK TIME: **6 minutes**

This Indonesian salad is called Gado Gado—meaning "mix mix"—because it's made with a mixture of vegetables. It reminds me of a combination of a niçoise salad and a chopped Thai salad. It's usually made with potatoes, green beans, and a hardboiled egg like a niçoise salad, and it's served with a peanut dressing, similar to a Thai salad. Recipes vary by region and can be altered to suit personal tastes, so feel free to play with the ingredients. Tempeh can be used in place of the baked tofu, and broccoli can be used instead of green beans.

1 small sweet potato, diced into
   1-inch pieces

½ pound green beans, trimmed

3 cups thinly sliced red (or green) cabbage

1 cup mung bean sprouts

1 medium cucumber, chopped

4 medium radishes, thinly sliced

8 ounces Baked Tofu (see page 28), or
   store-bought baked tofu

Spicy Peanut Dressing (see page 26), or
   store-bought spicy peanut dressing

2 scallions, sliced

1. Prepare a large bowl with ice water and bring a large pot of salted water to a boil. Add the sweet potatoes to the boiling water and cook for 4 minutes. Add the green beans to the pot with the potatoes and continue to cook for 2 more minutes. The sweet potatoes should be fork-tender, and the green beans should be bright green.

2. Remove the vegetables from the pot with a skimmer or slotted spoon and immediately transfer them to the ice water bowl. Let them sit in the ice water for a minute. Drain the vegetables, place them on a plate or cutting board, and pat them dry with a towel.

3. In a large bowl, toss together the cabbage, mung bean sprouts, cucumber, radishes, green beans, and sweet potatoes and baked tofu. Pour the Spicy Peanut Dressing over the salad and toss to combine everything. Top with the sliced scallions.

Slow it down: If you have a little extra time on your hands, you can roast the sweet potatoes. Toss the pieces in a little oil or aquafaba (the water from a can of chickpeas) along with a sprinkling of salt and pepper and bake them in a 400°F oven for about 20 minutes.

Per serving: Calories: 315; Total fat: 19g; Total carbs: 25g; Fiber: 7g; Sugar: 8g; Protein: 17g; Sodium: 243mg

Vegetable Curry, 79

CHAPTER FIVE

SOUPS AND STEWS

TOMATO SOUP

GLUTEN-FREE | LOW-CARB | NUT-FREE | SOY-FREE, OIL-FREE OPTION

SERVES 4 | PREP TIME: 10 minutes | COOK TIME: 25 minutes

I doubt there's a more classic soup than tomato. When I was little, tomato soup and grilled cheese sandwiches were a must-have meal on a cold winter's day. I grew up eating the canned stuff, which is loaded with sugar, but this homemade version doesn't take much effort and is made with simple, healthy ingredients. If you have some on hand, fresh basil or thyme would make a flavorful addition.

1 teaspoon neutral-flavored oil (such as grapeseed or avocado)

1 small onion, diced

2 garlic cloves, minced

1 (28-ounce) can diced tomatoes with their juices

4 cups Homemade Vegetable Stock (see page 20), or store-bought vegetable stock

Sea salt

Black pepper

1. Heat the oil in a large stockpot over medium-high heat. Add the onion and cook for about 5 minutes, until it has softened and begun to brown slightly. Add the garlic and cook for another 1 to 2 minutes.

2. Add the diced tomatoes with their juices and Homemade Vegetable Stock to the pot. Bring to a boil, and then reduce the heat to medium-low and cover the pot. Simmer for about 15 minutes. Remove the pot from heat.

3. Use an immersion blender to blend the soup in the pot until smooth and creamy. If you don't have an immersion blender, let the soup cool slightly, and then pour it into an upright blender or food processor and process until it's smooth and creamy. This may need to be done in batches if your blender is on the smaller side.

4. Pour the soup back into the pot. Place the pot back on the stove to simmer for about 5 more minutes, or until heated throughout. Season with sea salt and black pepper to taste.

Slow it down: If you have the time, this soup can be cooked in a slow cooker on low for 7 to 8 hours.

Substitution tip: Try using my Homemade Vegetable Stock or water in place of the neutral-flavored oil.

Per serving: Calories: 75; Total fat: 1g; Total carbs: 12g; Fiber: 3g; Sugar: 8g; Protein: 2g; Sodium: 312mg

MINESTRONE SOUP

GLUTEN-FREE OPTION | NUT-FREE | SOY-FREE, OIL-FREE OPTION

SERVES 6 | PREP TIME: 10 minutes | COOK TIME: 25 minutes

Minestrone is a classic Italian soup made with vegetables, beans, and pasta or rice. It more than likely originated as a creative method of making use of leftovers, with scraps and bits of food from other meals thrown into a big pot. Keeping with this tradition, it is a great way to clean out the refrigerator and use up the stray bits of veggies that are hanging around in the produce drawer.

1 teaspoon neutral-flavored oil (such as grapeseed or avocado)

1 medium onion, diced

2 carrots, chopped

2 celery stalks, chopped

3 garlic cloves, minced

4 cups Homemade Vegetable Stock (see page 20), or store-bought vegetable stock

1 (14-ounce) can diced tomatoes, with their liquid

1 (15-ounce) can cannellini, great northern, or navy beans, drained and rinsed

1 cup small whole-grain or gluten-free pasta (such as small shell or elbows)

1 large zucchini (or summer) squash, chopped

2 cups chopped kale, Swiss chard, or collard greens

½ teaspoon dried oregano

½ teaspoon dried thyme

¼ teaspoon red pepper flakes

1 tablespoon lemon juice

Sea salt

Black pepper

1. Heat the oil in a large stockpot over medium-high heat. Add the onion, carrots, and celery. Cook for about 5 minutes, until the vegetables are soft and have browned slightly. Add the garlic and cook for another 1 to 2 minutes.

2. Stir in the Homemade Vegetable Stock and diced tomatoes with their liquid. Bring the mixture to a boil, then add the beans, pasta, zucchini, leafy greens, oregano, thyme, and red pepper flakes. Reduce the heat to medium-low, cover the pot and let the soup simmer for about 10 minutes, or until the pasta is cooked al dente and the greens are tender.

3. Remove the pot from heat. Add the lemon juice and season with sea salt and black pepper to taste.

Substitution tip: If winter squash is in season, you can add it to the soup in the place of zucchini or summer squash. Use two cups of cubed butternut or acorn squash. The soup may need to simmer longer to allow the squash to soften. Also, try using my Homemade Vegetable Stock or water in place of the neutral-flavored oil.

Per serving: Calories: 153; Total fat: 1g; Total carbs: 31g; Fiber: 9g; Sugar: 6g; Protein: 7g; Sodium: 285mg

POTATO LEEK SOUP

GLUTEN-FREE | NUT-FREE | SOY-FREE, OIL-FREE OPTION

SERVES 4 | PREP TIME: 10 minutes | COOK TIME: 30 minutes

This soup is rich and creamy, without containing any actual cream. I usually make this soup with two potatoes, but I've gotten sneaky this time and added a little cauliflower in the place of one of them. The florets blend in nicely, and no one will be the wiser. Garnish this soup with fresh thyme or chives, if you happen to have some on hand.

1 teaspoon neutral-flavored oil (such as grapeseed or avocado)

2 leeks, white parts only, chopped

2 cups chopped cauliflower florets

1 medium russet potato, chopped

4 cups Homemade Vegetable Stock (see page 20), or store-bought vegetable stock

½ cup plain, unsweetened nondairy milk (such as almond or soy)

Sea salt

Black pepper

1. Heat the oil in a large stockpot over medium-high heat. Add the leeks and cook, stirring occasionally, for about 5 minutes, until they begin to brown.

2. Add the cauliflower, potatoes, and Homemade Vegetable Stock to the pot and bring to a boil. Reduce the heat to medium-low and cover the pot. Simmer for about 15 minutes, or until the potatoes are fork-tender. Remove the pot from heat and add the nondairy milk.

3. Use an immersion blender to blend the soup in the pot until smooth and creamy. If you don't have an immersion blender, let the soup cool slightly, and then pour it into an upright blender or food processor and process until it's smooth and creamy. This may need to be done in batches, if your blender is on the smaller side. Pour the soup back into the pot.

4. Place the pot back on the stove to simmer for about 5 more minutes, until heated throughout. Season with sea salt and black pepper to taste.

Prep tip: Leeks can be very dirty, hiding grit and sand in their many rings. Clean them by slicing them and placing them in a large bowl of water. Swish the leek pieces around a little, and then let them sit for 5 to 10 minutes while you prepare the rest of the recipe. The dirt will sink to the bottom of the bowl, and the leek pieces will float to the top. Then remove the leeks with a slotted spoon.

Substitution tip: Try using my Homemade Vegetable Stock or water in place of the neutral-flavored oil.

Per serving: Calories: 148; Total fat: 1g; Total carbs: 33g; Fiber: 4g; Sugar: 5g; Protein: 4g; Sodium: 261mg

SPLIT PEA SOUP

GLUTEN-FREE | NUT-FREE | SOY-FREE, OIL-FREE OPTION

SERVES 4 | PREP TIME: 10 minutes | COOK TIME: 90 minutes

Split pea is probably my favorite type of soup. In the past, I didn't have the patience to cook my own, so I would buy containers of it premade from the grocery store—until the day I happened to notice the price of a bag of split peas. A one-pound bag was a fraction of the cost of the premade soup. So, I bought the peas and started making it myself. It comes together quickly, but it does need to simmer for a while to allow the peas to soften.

1 teaspoon neutral-flavored oil (such as grapeseed or avocado)

1 medium onion, diced

3 medium carrots, chopped

2 celery stalks, chopped

3 garlic cloves, minced

5 cups Homemade Vegetable Stock (see page 20), or store-bought vegetable stock

1 bay leaf

1½ cups dried split peas, rinsed (see tip on page 71)

1 teaspoon dried thyme

1 teaspoon smoked paprika

½ teaspoon sea salt

½ teaspoon black pepper

1. Heat the oil in a large stockpot over medium-high heat. Add the onion, carrots, and celery. Cook, stirring frequently, for about 8 minutes, until the vegetables are soft and have browned slightly. Add the garlic and cook for 2 more minutes.

2. Add the Homemade Vegetable Stock, bay leaf, split peas, thyme, smoked paprika, sea salt, and black pepper to the pot. Bring to a boil and then reduce the heat to medium-low.

3. Cover the pot and let the soup simmer, stirring occasionally for 60 to 70 minutes, or until the peas have softened and the soup has reached the desired consistency. Remove the bay leaf before serving.

Ingredient tip: Before adding the split peas to the pot, place them in a colander to make sure there aren't any pebbles or other foreign items within, and then give them a good rinse.

Substitution tip: Try using my Homemade Vegetable Stock or water in place of the neutral-flavored oil.

Per serving: Calories: 249; Total fat: 4g; Total carbs: 45g; Fiber: 17g; Sugar: 10g; Protein: 15g; Sodium: 249mg

CHEESY BROCCOLI SOUP

GLUTEN-FREE | LOW-CARB | OIL-FREE | SOY-FREE

SERVES 4 | PREP TIME: 5 minutes | COOK TIME: 15 minutes

Growing up, I loved the combination of broccoli and cheddar, but as a vegan with dairy sensitivities, that cheesy soup was off limits. Since I discovered that boiled vegetables can be blended together with a few other ingredients to create a nondairy cheesy sauce, veganized broccoli cheddar soup has been a regular addition to my diet. I've blanched the broccoli here, but you can also steam or roast it.

4 cups Cheesy Vegetable Sauce (see page 24)

½ cup Homemade Vegetable Stock (see page 20), or store-bought vegetable stock

4 cups broccoli florets, chopped into small pieces

Sea salt

Black pepper

Make-ahead tip: The Cheesy Vegetable Sauce (skipping the simmering step) and broccoli can be prepared in advance and then cooked just before you're ready to eat.

Per serving: Calories: 263; Total fat: 0g; Total carbs: 28g; Fiber: 11g; Sugar: 6g; Protein: 19g; Sodium: 454mg

1. Prepare a large bowl with ice water and bring a large pot of salted water to a boil. Add the broccoli to the boiling water and cook for about 3 minutes, or until it's bright green.

2. Remove the broccoli from the pot with tongs or a skimmer, and immediately transfer it to the ice water bowl. Let it sit in the ice water for a minute. Remove the broccoli from the water.

3. Heat the Cheesy Vegetable Sauce and Homemade Vegetable Stock in a large stockpot over medium-high heat. Add the broccoli and bring to a boil. Reduce the heat to medium-low and simmer for about 10 minutes, or until the soup is heated throughout. If the soup becomes too thick, add a little more stock until it reaches the desired consistency. Season with sea salt and black pepper to taste.

MUSHROOM BARLEY SOUP

GLUTEN-FREE | LOW-CARB | NUT-FREE | SOY-FREE, OIL-FREE OPTION

SERVES 4 | PREP TIME: **10 minutes** | COOK TIME: **50 minutes**

Most mushroom barley soups are made with pearl barley, which is not actually a whole grain. It has been polished to remove the outer bran and endosperm layers. This recipe calls for whole grain hulled barley, which has intact bran and endosperm layers. Hulled barley takes a little longer to cook than pearled, but it's worth it. It's chewier and doesn't retain as much liquid, so it will have an al dente feel when it's done. If you're sensitive to gluten, you can use brown rice in place of the barley.

1 teaspoon neutral-flavored oil (such as grapeseed or avocado)

1 medium onion, diced

2 medium carrots, chopped

2 celery stalks, chopped

12 ounces cremini mushrooms (or white button mushrooms), sliced

4 cups Homemade Vegetable Stock (see page 20), or store-bought vegetable stock

½ cup hulled barley

Sea salt

Black pepper

Slow it down: If you have the time, this soup can be cooked in a slow cooker on low for 6 to 8 hours.

Substitution tip: Try using my Homemade Vegetable Stock or water in place of the neutral-flavored oil.

Per serving: Calories: 117; Total fat: 2g; Total carbs: 22g; Fiber: 6g; Sugar: 6g; Protein: 5g; Sodium: 259mg

1. Heat the oil in a large stockpot over medium-high heat. Add the onion, carrots, celery, and mushrooms and cook, stirring occasionally, for about 5 minutes, until the vegetables begin to soften.

2. Add the Homemade Vegetable Stock and barley and bring the soup to a boil. Reduce the heat to medium-low. Cover the pot and simmer, stirring occasionally, for 40 to 45 minutes, until the barley is soft and chewy. Season with sea salt and black pepper to taste.

LENTIL SOUP

GLUTEN-FREE | NUT-FREE | SOY-FREE, OIL-FREE OPTION

SERVES 4 | PREP TIME: 10 minutes | COOK TIME: 30 minutes

This recipe is kind of a choose-your-own-adventure soup because the type of lentils you use is up to you. Brown or green lentils have a meaty texture and don't break apart easily. Cooking with them will result in a hearty, almost stew-like soup. Quick-cooking red lentils are more delicate and will nearly disintegrate when cooking, creating a thick, almost creamy soup.

1 teaspoon neutral-flavored oil (such as grapeseed or avocado)

1 medium onion, diced

1 medium carrot, chopped

2 celery stalks, chopped

2 garlic cloves, minced

1 cup dried lentils

1 (14-ounce) can crushed tomatoes

4 cups Homemade Vegetable Stock (see page 20), or store-bought vegetable stock

2 cups finely chopped kale

1 tablespoon lemon juice

Sea salt

Black pepper

Ingredient tip: Much like split peas, lentils need to be sorted through before cooking. To do so, place them in a colander and check to make sure there aren't any pebbles or other foreign items present. Rinse them before adding them to the soup.

Substitution tip: Try using my Homemade Vegetable Stock or water in place of the neutral-flavored oil.

Per serving: Calories: 272; Total fat: 2g; Total carbs: 49g; Fiber: 20g; Sugar: 10g; Protein: 16g; Sodium: 318mg

1. Heat the oil in a large stockpot over medium-high heat. Add the onion, carrots, and celery and cook, stirring occasionally, for about 5 minutes, until the vegetables begin to soften. Add the garlic and cook for another 1 to 2 minutes.

2. Add the lentils, crushed tomatoes, and Homemade Vegetable Stock to the pot. Bring the soup to a boil. Reduce the heat to medium-low. Cover the pot and simmer, stirring occasionally, for about 20 minutes, until the lentils soften.

3. Bring the heat up to medium, add the kale to the pot, and stir to combine. Cook, stirring frequently, for about 5 minutes, until the kale has wilted.

4. Remove the pot from heat and stir in the lemon juice. Season with sea salt and black pepper to taste.

VEGETABLE CHILI

GLUTEN-FREE | NUT-FREE | SOY-FREE

SERVES 8 | PREP TIME: 15 minutes | COOK TIME: 30 minutes

When I worked in an office, one of my coworkers thought it would be fun to have a chili cookoff. Some made meaty chilis, and I served my vegan version. There was no voting, so there was no actual winner, but a few people came up to me afterward and told me they liked mine the best. So, don't be afraid to whip up this version at your next event. Serve this chili in large bowls, topped with sprigs of cilantro, chopped scallions, slices of jalapeño peppers, or diced avocado. It's also fantastic served over a baked sweet potato.

1 teaspoon neutral-flavored oil (such as grapeseed or avocado)

1 medium red onion, diced

3 garlic cloves, minced

2 carrots, chopped

1 poblano pepper, chopped

1 red bell pepper, chopped

1 medium zucchini, diced

2 cups Hearty Veggie Crumbles (see page 29)

2 cups Homemade Vegetable Stock (see page 20), or store-bought vegetable stock

1 (28-ounce) can crushed tomatoes

1 (15-ounce) can pinto beans, drained and rinsed

1 (15-ounce) can black beans, drained and rinsed

2 teaspoons chili powder

2 teaspoons cumin

1 teaspoon garlic powder

1 teaspoon onion powder

½ teaspoon cayenne pepper

½ teaspoon sea salt

½ teaspoon black pepper

1. Heat the oil in a large stockpot over medium-high heat. Add the onion and garlic and cook for about 5 minutes, until they begin to brown. Add the carrots, poblano pepper, bell pepper, and zucchini, and continue to cook for 10 to 15 minutes, until they soften, stirring frequently.

2. Add the Hearty Veggie Crumbles, Homemade Vegetable Stock, crushed tomatoes, pinto beans, black beans, chili powder, cumin, garlic powder, onion powder, cayenne pepper, sea salt, and black pepper. Reduce the heat to medium-low and simmer, stirring occasionally, for about 10 minutes, until heated throughout.

CONTINUED

Substitution tip: Feel free to play with the vegetables and beans in this dish. If you prefer kidney beans over pinto, they'll work just as well. Celery and fresh corn would be just as tasty as carrots and zucchini. Also, try using my Homemade Vegetable Stock or water in place of the neutral-flavored oil.

Per serving: Calories: 319; Total fat: 2g; Total carbs: 58g; Fiber: 16g; Sugar: 10g; Protein: 21g; Sodium: 289mg

PEANUT STEW

GLUTEN-FREE | SOY-FREE

SERVES 6 | PREP TIME: 10 minutes | COOK TIME: 25 minutes

Peanut stew, also called groundnut stew, is a staple food in Western Africa. Recipes for it vary, but it's usually made with a paste made from peanuts, tomatoes, onion, garlic, and leafy greens or root vegetables. Sweet potato and eggplant lend themselves well to this stew, but it's also delicious with winter squash and okra. It can be served with or without cooked brown rice or my Cauliflower Rice (see page 22).

1 teaspoon neutral-flavored oil (such as grapeseed or avocado)

1 medium yellow onion, diced

3 garlic cloves, minced

1 tablespoon grated or minced fresh ginger

2 cups Homemade Vegetable Stock (see page 20), or store-bought vegetable stock

1 (14-ounce) can diced tomatoes with their juices

½ cup natural creamy peanut butter

1 medium sweet potato, chopped

1 medium eggplant, peeled and chopped

1 (15-ounce) can kidney beans, drained and rinsed

1 teaspoon cumin

1 teaspoon coriander

½ teaspoon red pepper flakes

3 cups chopped collard greens (or kale)

Sea salt

Black pepper

¼ cup unsalted, roasted peanuts, chopped

1. Heat the oil in a large stockpot over medium-high heat. Add the onion, garlic, and ginger and cook for about 5 minutes, until they begin to brown.

2. Add the Homemade Vegetable Stock, diced tomatoes with their juices, and peanut butter and stir to combine.

3. Add the sweet potato, eggplant, kidney beans, cumin, coriander, and red pepper flakes to the pot, and stir to combine. Bring the stew to a boil, and then reduce the heat to medium-low, cover the pot and simmer, stirring occasionally, for about 15 minutes, or until the sweet potato has softened.

CONTINUED

4. Bring the heat up to medium, add the collard greens to the pot and stir to combine. Cook, stirring frequently, until the greens have wilted. Season with sea salt and black pepper to taste, and garnish with chopped peanuts.

Slow it down: This soup can be prepared in a slow cooker. Cook all of the ingredients with the exception of the greens on low for 5 to 6 hours. Stir in the greens and cook for another hour.

Substitution tip: Try using my Homemade Vegetable Stock or water in place of the neutral-flavored oil.

Per serving: Calories: 306; Total fat: 14g; Total carbs: 35g; Fiber: 10g; Sugar: 8g; Protein: 15g; Sodium: 173mg

VEGETABLE CURRY

GLUTEN-FREE | LOW-CARB | NUT-FREE | SOY-FREE

SERVES 6 | PREP TIME: 10 minutes | COOK TIME: 20 minutes

Vegetable curries are a favorite warming meal on cold days. I tend to make them with whatever stray bits of vegetables I have on hand to clean out the produce drawer of the refrigerator, but this combination of cauliflower, green beans, and carrots is my personal favorite. This is a Thai-style curry that uses red curry paste, but it can also be made with the green variety.

1 teaspoon neutral-flavored oil (such as grapeseed or avocado)

1 medium yellow onion, diced

3 garlic cloves, minced

1 tablespoon grated or minced fresh ginger

1 (14-ounce) can light coconut milk

1 cup Homemade Vegetable Stock (see page 20), or store-bought vegetable stock

3 tablespoons red curry paste (see Ingredient tip)

4 cups chopped cauliflower florets

½ pound green beans, trimmed and cut into 1-inch pieces

2 carrots, chopped

1 (15-ounce) can chickpeas, drained and rinsed

2 cups spinach

Sea salt

Black pepper

Substitution tip: Try using my Homemade Vegetable Stock or water in place of the neutral-flavored oil.

Per serving: Calories: 192; Total fat: 7g; Total carbs: 28g; Fiber: 7g; Sugar: 8g; Protein: 7g; Sodium: 324mg

1. Heat the oil in a large stockpot over medium-high heat. Add the onion, garlic, and ginger and cook for about 5 minutes, until they begin to brown.

2. Add the light coconut milk, Homemade Vegetable Stock, and red curry paste to the pot and stir to combine. Add the cauliflower, green beans, carrots, and chickpeas. Bring the mixture to a boil, and then reduce the heat to medium-low. Cover the pot and simmer for about 15 minutes, or until the vegetables have softened.

3. Uncover the pot and stir in the spinach, continuing to simmer, while stirring frequently until the spinach wilts. Season with sea salt and black pepper to taste.

Cauliflower Bánh Mì, 91

CHAPTER SIX

BURGERS, SANDWICHES, AND WRAPS

NO-BEAN HUMMUS WRAPS

GLUTEN-FREE OPTION | NUT-FREE | OIL-FREE | SOY-FREE

SERVES 6 | PREP TIME: 10 minutes

Hummus is traditionally made with chickpeas, but I've snuck a zucchini into their place here; because much of the flavor comes from tahini and lemon juice, I doubt anyone will notice. I've included my favorite wrap fillings in this recipe, but you can use almost any fresh vegetables you'd like. Mixed greens, cut cucumber, and sliced tomatoes would be great additions.

FOR THE HUMMUS:

1 small zucchini, chopped
⅓ cup tahini
3 tablespoons lemon juice
1 garlic clove, minced
½ teaspoon sea salt

FOR THE WRAPS:

3 cups fresh spinach leaves, loosely packed
2 carrots, shredded or grated
1 cup pea shoots (or bean sprouts)
1 bell pepper, cut into thin strips
1 large avocado, sliced
6 large (12-inch) whole-grain (or gluten-free) wraps, flatbreads, or tortillas

1. To make the hummus: Combine the zucchini, tahini, lemon juice, garlic, and sea salt together in a food processor or blender and blend until smooth and creamy. If it's too thick, add water, 1 teaspoon at a time.

2. To make the wraps: Spoon the hummus down the center of each wrap. Top each with the spinach leaves, shredded carrots, pea shoots, bell pepper strips, avocado slices. Roll the wrap, tucking in the sides as you go.

Substitution tip: If you'd like to get uber-healthy with this recipe, use collard greens as wraps. To do so, you'll need four large collard leaves. Cut the stem off of each and use a sharp knife to carefully shave off the thick part of the stem from the back of each leaf. This will make them easier to roll.

Per serving: Calories: 407; Total fat: 20g; Total carbs: 47g; Fiber: 6g; Sugar: 3g; Protein: 11g; Sodium: 501mg

CHICKPEA SALAD SANDWICHES

GLUTEN-FREE OPTION | OIL-FREE | SOY-FREE

SERVES 4 | PREP TIME: **15 minutes**

Chickpea salad is one of the first vegan recipes many people learn to make. It's usually considered a tuna salad replacement, but here I've prepared it like Sonoma chicken salad and added celery, grapes, and pecans. I've used my Tahini Dressing instead of the traditional mayonnaise, which is loaded with oil. It can be served on a wrap or in a pita instead of bread. If you'd like to go old school, serve it in lettuce cups.

1 (15-ounce) can chickpeas, drained and rinsed

2 celery stalks, chopped

¾ cup seedless red grapes, sliced in half

¼ cup toasted pecans, coarsely chopped

½ cup Tahini Dressing (see page 25)

Sea salt

Black pepper

8 slices of whole grain (or gluten-free) bread

1 large tomato, sliced

8 large lettuce leaves, chopped

1. In a large bowl, mash the chickpeas with a fork or potato masher. Add the celery, grapes, and pecans and mix to combine. Gently fold in the Tahini Dressing. Add sea salt and pepper to taste.

2. Serve on bread with sliced tomatoes and lettuce.

Substitution tip: It's easy to hide different kinds of veggies in this chickpea salad. Instead of what I've listed here, you can use diced carrots, diced bell peppers, and sliced scallions. Feel free to play with add-ins.

Per serving: Calories: 440; Total fat: 17g; Total carbs: 56g; Fiber: 12g; Sugar: 13g; Protein: 17g; Sodium: 314mg

CAESAR CHICKPEA WRAPS

GLUTEN-FREE OPTION | NUT-FREE | OIL-FREE

SERVES 4 | PREP TIME: **10 minutes**

Caesar salad dressing was one of my favorites in my vegetarian days—until I took a look at the ingredients and realized that it was made with anchovies. This vegan version uses capers to mimic the briny taste of anchovies, and it gets its creamy texture from silken tofu. Besides being a tasty addition to this wrap, my Caesar Chickpeas are also great on salads. Collard green leaves can be used instead of tortillas (see tip on page 82).

FOR THE CAESAR DRESSING:

½ cup silken tofu

2 tablespoons lemon juice

1 teaspoon capers

½ teaspoon Dijon mustard

½ teaspoon garlic powder

½ teaspoon sea salt

FOR THE WRAPS:

1 (15-ounce) can chickpeas, drained and rinsed

6 cups shredded romaine lettuce

1 large carrot, shredded or grated

1 large tomato, sliced

4 large (12-inch) whole-grain (or gluten-free) wraps, flatbreads, or tortillas

1. To make the Caesar dressing: Combine the dressing ingredients together in a food processor or blender and blend until smooth and creamy.

2. To make the wraps: In a large bowl, combine the chickpeas, lettuce, carrot, and Caesar dressing. Stir to coat everything well.

3. Spoon the mixture down the center of each wrap. Top each with a couple tomato slices. Roll the tortilla up, tucking in the sides as you go.

Ingredient tip: Silken tofu can be found in shelf-stable, aseptic packages or in refrigerated, water-packed tubs. Either type can be used here. Use the remainder of the package in a smoothie or a creamy dip.

Per serving: Calories: 364; Total fat: 9g; Total carbs: 58g; Fiber: 7g; Sugar: 6g; Protein: 13g; Sodium: 430mg

TEMPEH LETTUCE WRAPS

....
GLUTEN-FREE OPTION | LOW-CARB | OIL-FREE OPTION
....

SERVES 4 | PREP TIME: 10 minutes | COOK TIME: 15 minutes

I like to make recipes using crumbled tempeh in my cooking classes to show people who may be new to using tempeh how to prepare it. Crumbled tempeh pairs well with mushrooms, and even die-hard mushroom haters have told me that they really like these wraps. If the fermented flavor of tempeh bothers you, you can simmer it in a pan filled with my Homemade Vegetable Stock for about half an hour before using it in the recipe. Tempeh can also be steamed before cooking.

1 teaspoon neutral-flavored oil (such as grapeseed or avocado)

8 ounces cremini mushrooms (or white button mushrooms), finely chopped

1 (8-ounce) package tempeh, crumbled

½ cup Homemade Vegetable Stock (see page 20), or store-bought vegetable stock

¼ cup low-sodium tamari (or soy sauce)

2 tablespoons lime juice

2 tablespoons natural creamy peanut butter

½ teaspoon garlic powder

½ teaspoon ground ginger

½ teaspoon red pepper flakes

12 to 16 large Bibb lettuce (or butter lettuce) leaves

2 scallions, thinly sliced

½ cucumber, chopped

1 carrot, grated or shredded

1. Heat the oil in a large sauté pan over medium-high heat. Add the mushrooms and crumbled tempeh and cook, stirring occasionally, for about 10 minutes, until the mushrooms soften and the tempeh browns.

2. While the mushrooms and tempeh are cooking, whisk together the Homemade Vegetable Stock, tamari, lime juice, peanut butter, garlic powder, ground ginger, and red pepper flakes in a small bowl.

CONTINUED

3. Pour the sauce mixture into the pan, stir well to coat everything, and continue cooking for about 5 minutes, until the sauce thickens.

4. To serve, place a large spoonful of the mushroom and tempeh mixture onto each lettuce leaf and top with scallions, cucumber, and grated carrot. Roll up the lettuce leaves.

Speed it up: Using a food processor to chop the mushrooms can save a lot of prep time. It also cuts the mushrooms into smaller pieces that may be difficult to achieve by hand, making it easier to hide them from mushroom-haters.

Substitution tip: Try using my Homemade Vegetable Stock or water in place of the neutral-flavored oil.

Per serving: Calories: 206; Total fat: 10g; Total carbs: 17g; Fiber: 3g; Sugar: 4g; Protein: 16g; Sodium: 377mg

SWEET POTATO FALAFEL PITAS

GLUTEN-FREE OPTION | NUT-FREE | OIL-FREE | SOY-FREE

SERVES 4 | PREP TIME: 15 minutes | COOK TIME: 30 minutes

Falafel sandwiches have always been a favorite of mine. I bought my first one from a street-cart vendor in New York City, during my college days. I was newly vegetarian, and I knew they were meat-free. After a few bites, I was hooked! Falafel balls are usually deep-fried in oil, so they're not always the healthiest choice. In this recipe, they are baked, making them a more nutritious option. I've also added mashed sweet potato for a healthy twist.

1 cup parsley, packed

1 (15-ounce) can sweet potato purée (or 1 medium-size sweet potato), baked or steamed

1 (15-ounce) can chickpeas, drained and rinsed

2 cloves garlic, chopped

2 tablespoons tahini

1 teaspoon ground cumin

½ teaspoon sea salt

½ teaspoon black pepper

⅓ cup chickpea flour

4 whole-wheat (or gluten-free) pitas

1 tomato, sliced

½ small cucumber, sliced

8 to 10 lettuce leaves, chopped

½ cup Tahini Dressing (see page 25), for serving

1. Preheat your oven to 400°F and line a baking sheet with parchment paper.

2. Place the parsley in a food processor fitted with an s-blade. Pulse a few times, until the parsley is chopped.

3. Add the sweet potato, chickpeas, garlic, tahini, cumin, sea salt, and black pepper to the food processor. Process until everything is mixed together, and the mixture resembles a chunky paste. You may need to stop and scrape down the sides of your food processor once or twice. Pulse in the chickpea flour.

4. Use a melon-baller or large spoon to form the mixture into 16 small balls, about 1½ inches in diameter.

CONTINUED

5. Place the falafel balls on the prepared baking sheet and flatten them slightly with the back of a spoon. Bake for 25 to 30 minutes. Flip them at the halfway point to ensure even cooking. They should be golden brown and firm when done.

6. Place 4 falafel balls into each pita pocket along with the tomato slices, cucumber, and lettuce. Drizzle each pocket with about 2 tablespoons of tahini dressing.

Ingredient tip: Chickpea flour is used to help bind the mixture together. It can usually be found in the baking area of the grocery store, with the gluten-free flours. It is sometimes called garbanzo bean flour or besan. Whole-wheat flour, spelt flour, or oat flour can be used if chickpea flour isn't available.

Per serving: Calories: 485; Total fat: 16g; Total carbs: 72g; Fiber: 14g; Sugar: 7g; Protein: 18g; Sodium: 577mg

MUSHROOM PO' BOYS

GLUTEN-FREE OPTION | NUT-FREE OPTION | OIL-FREE | SOY-FREE OPTION

SERVES 4 | PREP TIME: **15 minutes** | COOK TIME: **30 minutes**

Traditionally made with roast beef or fried seafood, po' boy sandwiches hail from Louisiana. The first time I had one was at a vegan restaurant named Sprig and Vine in New Hope, Pennsylvania. I ordered it not knowing what it was—I just wanted the crispy oyster mushrooms. After a few bites, it was clear that I was experiencing a culinary miracle. Since then, I've had po' boys made with cauliflower, seitan, and tofu, but that oyster mushroom version that I first experienced remains my favorite.

¾ cup nondairy milk (such as soy or almond)

2 tablespoons cornstarch (or arrowroot)

1 cup cornmeal

2 teaspoons garlic powder

1 teaspoon onion powder

1 teaspoon paprika

½ teaspoon sea salt

½ teaspoon black pepper

¼ teaspoon cayenne pepper

8 ounces mushrooms (such as oyster, cremini, or white button), tough stems removed, sliced, if necessary

4 teaspoons hot sauce (such as Tabasco, Frank's, or Cholula)

4 teaspoons spicy mustard

4 (6-inch) whole grain (or gluten-free) submarine sandwich rolls or baguettes

2 large tomatoes, sliced

12 large lettuce leaves, chopped

¼ cup pickle slices

1. Preheat your oven to 400°F and line a baking sheet with parchment paper.

2. In a medium-size bowl, whisk together the nondairy milk and cornstarch. In another medium-size bowl, mix together the cornmeal, garlic powder, onion powder, paprika, sea salt, black pepper, and cayenne pepper.

3. Place the mushrooms in the bowl with the nondairy milk mixture and toss them to coat them well. Then place them in the bowl with the cornmeal mixture and toss to coat them well.

CONTINUED

4. Place the mushrooms on the prepared baking sheet and bake for about 30 minutes, or until crisp and golden brown, flipping them at the halfway point.

5. Spread the hot sauce and mustard onto each roll. Place a few mushrooms on each, and top with the tomato slices, lettuce, and pickles.

Speed it up: If you have an air fryer, you can air fry the mushrooms on 400°F for 20 minutes, flipping them after about 10 minutes.

Per serving: Calories: 422; Total fat: 7g; Total carbs: 78g; Fiber: 7g; Sugar: 9g; Protein: 15g; Sodium: 534mg

CAULIFLOWER BÁNH MÌ

GLUTEN-FREE OPTION | NUT-FREE | OIL-FREE OPTION

SERVES 4 | PREP TIME: **15 minutes** | COOK TIME: **10 minutes**

Bánh mì is the Vietnamese word for bread, and it also refers to a sandwich made with meat, cucumber, cilantro, pickled carrots, and daikon radishes. It is traditionally served with mayo and chilis on a baguette. The star of this vegan version is the spicy, pan-fried cauliflower, and I opted for carrots and radishes mixed with a little vinegar instead of pickled vegetables.

1 medium carrot, thinly sliced

4 medium radishes, thinly sliced

2 tablespoons rice vinegar (or apple cider vinegar)

¼ teaspoon sea salt

1 small head of cauliflower, leaves removed

1 teaspoon neutral-flavored oil (such as grapeseed or avocado)

2 tablespoons low-sodium tamari (or soy sauce)

1 teaspoon red pepper flakes

2 tablespoons tahini

2 tablespoons water, plus more if needed

1 tablespoon lime juice

1 tablespoon sriracha

4 (6-inch) whole grain (or gluten-free) submarine sandwich rolls or baguettes

1 medium cucumber, sliced

¼ cup pickled jalapeño slices

¼ cup chopped cilantro

1. In a medium bowl, toss together the carrot and radish slices with the rice vinegar and sea salt. Set aside until ready to use.

2. Place the cauliflower on a large cutting board, stem-side down, and slice it the way you would a loaf of bread into slices about ½-inch thick. Cut off any large pieces of the core and break apart very large pieces into smaller ones.

3. Heat the oil in a large sauté pan or cast-iron pan over medium-high heat. Place the cauliflower pieces in the pan, and drizzle with the tamari. Sprinkle with the red pepper flakes. Cook for about 5 minutes, until the bottom browns, and then flip the pieces and cook for another 5 minutes.

CONTINUED

4. In a small bowl, whisk together the tahini, water, lime juice, and sriracha.

5. Spoon the spicy tahini onto each roll. Place a few pieces of cauliflower on each, and top with the carrot and radish mixture, cucumber, pickled jalapeño, and cilantro.

Substitution tip: Sliced Baked Tofu (see page 28) can be used instead of cauliflower. Also, try using my Homemade Vegetable Stock (see page 20) or water in place of the neutral-flavored oil.

Per serving: Calories: 297; Total fat: 7g; Total carbs: 47g; Fiber: 7g; Sugar: 9g; Protein: 13g; Sodium: 456mg

LENTIL SLOPPY JOES

GLUTEN-FREE OPTION | NUT-FREE | OIL-FREE OPTION | SOY-FREE

SERVES 6 | PREP TIME: **10 minutes** | COOK TIME: **30 minutes**

Sloppy Joes were a favorite of mine when I was young. Back then, they were usually made with ground beef and canned Manwich® sauce. This vegan version uses lentils in the place of meat and an easy homemade sauce in place of the traditional canned choice. There are also a few veggies hidden in the mix, but I doubt anyone will notice them. This sandwich is deliciously messy, so make sure you have a stack of napkins nearby.

1 teaspoon neutral-flavored oil (such as grapeseed or avocado)

½ red onion, diced

2 cloves garlic, minced

5 ounces cremini mushrooms (or white button mushrooms), finely chopped

1 small zucchini, shredded or grated

1 red bell pepper, coarsely chopped

1 (15-ounce) can brown lentils, drained and rinsed

1½ cups Quick and Easy Tomato Sauce (see page 27) or store-bought tomato sauce

2 tablespoons maple syrup

1 tablespoon yellow mustard

2 teaspoons chili powder

½ teaspoon sea salt

6 whole-wheat (or gluten-free) buns, for serving

1. Heat the oil in a large sauté pan over medium-high heat. Add the onion and cook, stirring frequently, for about 5 minutes, or until it has softened and begun to brown. Add the garlic, mushrooms, zucchini, and bell pepper, and continue cooking, stirring frequently, for about 10 minutes, until the vegetables have softened.

2. Add the lentils, tomato sauce, maple syrup, mustard, chili powder, and sea salt to the pan. Bring to a boil. Reduce the heat to medium, and simmer uncovered for about 10 minutes, stirring frequently, until the tomato sauce has thickened slightly.

3. Spoon the mixture onto buns.

CONTINUED

Slow it down: If you'd prefer to start with dry lentils and cook them yourself, you'll need 3/4 cup of dried lentils. Place them in a large stockpot with 1¼ cups water over medium-high heat. Bring the water to a boil, and then reduce the heat to medium-low, cover the pot, and let it simmer for 20 minutes.

Substitution tip: Try using my Homemade Vegetable Stock (see page 20) or water in place of the neutral-flavored oil.

Per serving: Calories: 225; Total fat: 2g; Total carbs: 44g; Fiber: 7g; Sugar: 12g; Protein: 11g; Sodium: 342mg

BLACK BEAN BURGERS

GLUTEN-FREE OPTION | NUT-FREE | OIL-FREE OPTION | SOY-FREE

MAKES 6 burgers | PREP TIME: 15 minutes | COOK TIME: 24 minutes

These are anything but traditional black bean burgers, and you'll likely find your non-vegan guests wanting to join in on the delicious treat. There's no need to rinse the beans when making these burgers, as the bean water will help hold them together. The mushrooms aren't very noticeable, but they add a touch of flavor and a hearty texture. You can top these burgers with all your favorite burger fixings. To "super-size" them, pile on the pickles, grilled onions, avocado, mustard, and a little hot sauce.

1 teaspoon neutral-flavored oil (such as grapeseed or avocado)

5 ounces cremini mushrooms (or white button mushrooms), coarsely chopped

1 medium carrot, grated or shredded

1 (15-ounce) can black beans, drained

1 cup cooked brown rice

¼ cup rolled oats

¼ cup cornstarch (or arrowroot)

1 tablespoon tomato paste

1 garlic clove, minced

2 teaspoons chili powder

½ teaspoon black pepper

½ teaspoon sea salt

½ teaspoon red pepper flakes

6 whole-wheat (or gluten-free) burger buns

Tomato slices, for serving

Lettuce leaves, for serving

1. Preheat oven to 400°F and line a baking sheet with parchment paper.

2. Heat the oil in a large sauté pan over medium-high heat. Add the mushrooms and carrots and cook, stirring frequently, for about 10 minutes, or until they've softened and browned.

3. Place the mushrooms, carrots, black beans, rice, rolled oats, cornstarch, tomato paste, garlic, chili powder, black pepper, sea salt, and red pepper flakes in a food processor. Pulse until chopped and well-mixed. You may need to stop and scrape down the sides of the food processor once or twice. It's okay if the mixture is a little chunky.

CONTINUED

4. Divide the mixture into 6 equal pieces and shape each one into a patty. Place each patty onto the prepared baking sheet.

5. Bake the burgers for 10 to 12 minutes. Flip them and bake for an additional 10 to 12 minutes. They should be golden brown and firm.

6. Serve the burgers on whole-wheat buns with the tomato slices and lettuce leaves along with any other toppings you'd like.

Prep tip: If you don't have a food processor, you can combine the burger ingredients in a large bowl and mash everything together with a potato masher. The burgers will be a little chunkier than those made with a food processor, but they'll still be tasty.

Substitution tip: Try using my Homemade Vegetable Stock (see page 20) or water in place of the neutral-flavored oil.

Per serving: Calories: 341; Total fat: 3g; Total carbs: 69g; Fiber: 13g; Sugar: 8g; Protein: 15g; Sodium: 347mg

BEAN BALL SUBS

GLUTEN-FREE OPTION | OIL-FREE | SOY-FREE

SERVES **4** | PREP TIME: **15 minutes** | COOK TIME: **25 minutes**

I was never a big fan of meatballs, but I really enjoy meatless "meatballs" now that I'm vegan. This baked version is made with kidney beans, carrots, onion, walnuts, and rolled oats, and the recipe comes together quickly. I usually serve bean balls in a sandwich, but they can also be served with pasta or my Zucchini Noodles (see page 21).

¾ cup rolled oats

½ cup walnuts

1 (15-ounce) can kidney beans, drained and rinsed

1 medium carrot, grated or shredded

¼ cup minced onion

2 garlic cloves, minced

1 tablespoon tomato paste

1 teaspoon garlic powder

1 teaspoon onion powder

1 teaspoon dried thyme

1 teaspoon dried oregano

½ teaspoon sea salt

4 (6-inch) whole grain (or gluten-free) submarine sandwich rolls

4 cups Quick and Easy Tomato Sauce (see page 27) or store-bought tomato sauce

Substitution tip: Just about any type of cooked bean can be used in the place of kidney beans. Lentils, black beans, or chickpeas would work well.

Per serving: Calories: 460; Total fat: 13g; Total carbs: 73g; Fiber: 15g; Sugar: 9g; Protein: 19g; Sodium: 443mg

1. Preheat your oven to 400°F and line a baking sheet with parchment paper.

2. Grind the rolled oats and walnuts in a food processor into a course meal. Be careful not to overprocess them.

3. Add the kidney beans, carrot, onion, garlic, tomato paste, garlic powder, onion powder, thyme, oregano, and sea salt and pulse to combine everything.

4. Form the mixture into balls, 1 to 1½ inches in diameter. You should have 20 to 24 balls in total.

5. Bake the balls for 20 to 25 minutes, flipping them halfway through. They should be golden brown and firm.

6. To make the subs: Divide the bean balls among the rolls and top with the Quick and Easy Tomato Sauce.

Chili Lime Roasted Radishes, 105

CHAPTER SEVEN

SIDES

BAKED ZUCCHINI FRIES

GLUTEN-FREE OPTION | LOW-CARB | NUT-FREE OPTION | OIL-FREE | SOY-FREE OPTION

SERVES 4 | PREP TIME: 10 minutes | COOK TIME: 20 minutes

I used to live close to a diner and I'd often go there with friends for late-night munchies. I usually ordered a roasted vegetable sandwich with a side of zucchini fries. The fries were deep-fried in oil and not at all healthy, but I enjoyed them immensely. I've made a much more nutritious version of my old favorite by baking them in an oven. They're a terrific companion to just about any sandwich or burger, and they make a great appetizer when served with my warmed Quick and Easy Tomato Sauce (see page 27).

½ cup nondairy milk (such as soy or almond)

1 tablespoon cornstarch (or arrowroot)

1 cup whole-wheat (or gluten-free) bread crumbs

1 teaspoon garlic powder

1 teaspoon onion powder

1 teaspoon dried oregano

½ teaspoon sea salt

½ teaspoon black pepper

2 large zucchinis, ends trimmed and cut into thin strips (about 3 inches long and ½-inch thick)

Speed it up: If you have an air fryer, you can air fry your zucchini sticks on 400°F for 12 minutes, flipping them after 6 minutes.

Per serving: Calories: 66; Total fat: 2g; Total carbs: 12g; Fiber: 3g; Sugar: 3g; Protein: 3g; Sodium: 62mg

1. Preheat your oven to 425°F and line a baking sheet with parchment paper.

2. In a medium bowl, whisk together the nondairy milk and cornstarch. In another medium bowl, mix together the bread crumbs, garlic powder, onion powder, oregano, sea salt, and black pepper.

3. Dip the zucchini sticks in the bowl with the nondairy milk. Then dip them in the bowl with the bread crumb mixture, coating them well.

4. Place the zucchini sticks on the prepared baking sheet and bake them for about 20 minutes, or until crisp and golden brown, flipping them at the halfway point.

BLACK PEPPER MUSHROOMS

GLUTEN-FREE | LOW-CARB | NUT-FREE | OIL-FREE OPTION | SOY-FREE

SERVES 4 | PREP TIME: 10 minutes | COOK TIME: 15 minutes

Mushrooms are probably my favorite vegetable. I've had people tell me that they don't like them because of their texture, and I will admit that they do take some getting used to. But they're loaded with nutrients, so they're worth adding into your diet. Many varieties of mushrooms exist—each with its own nutritional profile—but, in general, they are good sources of many minerals, including potassium, zinc, and copper, as well as B vitamins, phytonutrients, and even protein.

1 teaspoon neutral-flavored oil (such as grapeseed or avocado)

16 ounces cremini mushrooms (or white button mushrooms), sliced

1 garlic clove, minced

1 tablespoon balsamic vinegar

1½ teaspoons black pepper

½ teaspoon sea salt

¼ teaspoon red pepper flakes

Ingredient tip: If, like me, you enjoy your mushrooms on the garlicky side, feel free to add another minced clove or two.

Substitution tip: Try using my Homemade Vegetable Stock (see page 20) or water in place of the neutral-flavored oil.

Per serving: Calories: 37; Total fat: 0g; Total carbs: 4g; Fiber: 1g; Sugar: 2g; Protein: 4g; Sodium: 241mg

Heat the oil in a large sauté pan over medium-high heat. Add the mushrooms and cook for 10 minutes, stirring frequently, until they have released their liquid and begun to brown. Add the garlic, balsamic vinegar, black pepper, sea salt, and red pepper flakes to the pan. Stir to coat the mushrooms. Continue cooking for 2 or 3 minutes, until the balsamic vinegar has reduced slightly.

SESAME-GARLIC GREEN BEANS

GLUTEN-FREE OPTION | LOW-CARB | NUT-FREE | OIL-FREE OPTION

SERVES 4 | PREP TIME: 10 minutes | COOK TIME: 10 minutes

Sesame and garlic give green beans an Asian feel in this easy-to-make recipe, and the flavors lend themselves to many different vegetables. Green beans are a good source of many vitamins—including C, K, and folate—and, since they're gentle on the digestive tract, they're good for those who suffer from digestive conditions. This simple side can easily be turned into a main dish by adding cubed Baked Tofu (see page 28) and serving it over cooked brown rice or my Cauliflower Rice (see page 22).

1 teaspoon neutral-flavored oil (such as grapeseed or avocado)

1 pound green beans, trimmed and chopped into 2-inch pieces

1 tablespoon low-sodium tamari (or soy sauce)

2 garlic cloves, minced

2 scallions, sliced

2 tablespoons sesame seeds

Sea salt

Black pepper

Ingredient tip: Green beans can sometimes be a chore to trim and chop, so I like to look for the pre-cut variety in the produce department.

Substitution tip: Try using my Homemade Vegetable Stock (see page 20) or water in place of the neutral-flavored oil.

Per serving: Calories: 78; Total fat: 4g; Total carbs: 11g; Fiber: 5g; Sugar: 2g; Protein: 3g; Sodium: 159mg

1. Heat the oil in a large sauté pan over medium-high heat. Add the green beans and cook, stirring frequently, for about 5 minutes, until they begin to soften.

2. Add the tamari, garlic, and scallions to the pan. Stir to coat the green beans, reduce the heat to medium, and cover the pan. Cook for about 5 minutes, until the green beans are crisp-tender. Remove the lid and add the sesame seeds to the pan. Stir to coat the green beans well. Season with sea salt and black pepper to taste.

BUFFALO BRUSSELS SPROUTS

GLUTEN-FREE OPTION | LOW-CARB | NUT-FREE OPTION | OIL-FREE | SOY-FREE OPTION

SERVES 4 | PREP TIME: 10 minutes | COOK TIME: 30 minutes

Cauliflower usually gets the glory when it comes to veganizing Buffalo wings, but I think it's high time that Brussels sprouts get some of the attention. Brussels sprouts are highly versatile, and they're quite delicious when cooked properly. They're part of the cabbage family, which is known for helping reduce the risk of cancer. Brussels sprouts are an excellent source of nutrients, including vitamins C and K, folic acid, beta-carotene, and phytonutrients.

½ cup whole-grain flour (such as whole-wheat, spelt, or oat)

1 tablespoon cornstarch (or arrowroot)

1 teaspoon garlic powder

1 teaspoon onion powder

¼ teaspoon sea salt

½ cup plain, unsweetened nondairy milk (such as soy or almond)

1 pound Brussels sprouts, trimmed and cut in half

⅓ cup Homemade Vegetable Stock (see page 20), or aquafaba (the liquid from a can of chickpeas)

⅓ cup hot sauce (such as Tabasco, Frank's, or Cholula)

Prep tip: To prepare the Brussels sprouts, rinse them in a large colander, removing any brown or damaged outer leaves. Trim off the tough stem and cut each sprout in half.

Per serving: Calories: 126; Total fat: 1g; Total carbs: 26g; Fiber: 5g; Sugar: 3g; Protein: 6g; Sodium: 283mg

1. Preheat your oven to 400°F and line a baking sheet with parchment paper.

2. In a large bowl, whisk together the flour, cornstarch, garlic powder, onion powder, and sea salt. Slowly whisk in the nondairy milk. Toss the Brussels sprouts in the mixture, and then lay them out in a single layer on the prepared baking sheet.

3. Bake for 25 minutes, flipping them about halfway through.

4. While the Brussels sprouts are baking, whisk together the Homemade Vegetable Stock and hot sauce.

5. Remove the Brussels sprouts from the oven and brush them with the hot sauce mixture. Bake for 5 more minutes.

CREAMED KALE

GLUTEN-FREE | LOW-CARB | NUT-FREE | OIL-FREE OPTION | SOY-FREE

SERVES 4 | PREP TIME: **10 minutes** | COOK TIME: **17 minutes**

I've made creamed kale in some of the cooking classes that I teach, and self-proclaimed kale haters have told me that they loved it. But let's face it: A creamy sauce will make just about any disliked vegetable more palatable. This recipe is a great way to get picky eaters to eat their greens. Kale is probably one of the most nutritious vegetables on the planet, and it's a good source of vitamins and minerals including vitamins B, C, and E; copper; iron; and calcium. This dish pairs well with my Cauliflower Steaks with Spinach Pesto (see page 118) and Shepherdess's Pie with Sweet Potato Crust (see page 126).

1 teaspoon neutral-flavored oil (such as grapeseed or avocado)

¼ cup chopped onion

2 garlic cloves, minced

12 ounces curly kale, tough stems removed, chopped

¼ cup Homemade Vegetable Stock (see page 20), or store-bought vegetable stock

2 cups Creamy Cauliflower Sauce (see page 23)

1 tablespoon lemon juice

Substitution tip: Chard can be used instead of kale in this recipe. Also, try using my Homemade Vegetable Stock or water in place of the neutral-flavored oil.

Per serving: Calories: 74; Total fat: 1g; Total carbs: 14g; Fiber: 4g; Sugar: 3g; Protein: 4g; Sodium: 303mg

1. Heat the oil in a large sauté pan over medium-high heat. Add the onion and cook for about 5 minutes, until it has softened and begun to brown slightly. Add the garlic and cook for another 1 to 2 minutes.

2. Add the kale and Homemade Vegetable Stock to the pan and cook, stirring frequently, for about 5 minutes, until the kale begins to wilt.

3. Add the Creamy Cauliflower Sauce to the pan and stir to coat the kale well. Continue cooking over medium-high heat, stirring occasionally, for about 5 minutes, until the sauce is heated throughout.

4. Remove the pan from heat and stir in the lemon juice.

CHILI LIME ROASTED RADISHES

GLUTEN-FREE | LOW-CARB | NUT-FREE | OIL-FREE OPTION | SOY-FREE

SERVES 4 | PREP TIME: **10 minutes** | COOK TIME: **25 minutes**

Most people don't think of radishes when they roast vegetables for a side dish, but it's time we changed that. Roasting them mellows their bite, making them tender and juicy. Unlike with other veggies, the color of radishes tends to become more vibrant after 20 minutes in the oven, making this dish a lively addition to the dinner table. Radishes are a member of the cruciferous vegetable family, along with cabbage and kale, which means that they are low-calorie and rich in folate; potassium; vitamins C, E, and K; and fiber.

1½ pounds radishes, trimmed and cut in half

2 tablespoons lime juice

1 teaspoon neutral-flavored oil (such as grapeseed or avocado)

1 teaspoon chili powder

½ teaspoon sea salt

Speed it up: Radishes can be "roasted" in an air fryer. Cook them on 400°F for 12 to 15 minutes, shaking the basket after about 6 minutes.

Substitution tip: Try using my Homemade Vegetable Stock (see page 20) or water in place of the neutral-flavored oil.

Per serving: Calories: 45; Total fat: 1g; Total carbs: 8g; Fiber: 3g; Sugar: 4g; Protein: 1g; Sodium: 207mg

1. Preheat your oven to 400°F and line a baking sheet with parchment paper.

2. Place the radishes in a large bowl with the lime juice, oil, chili powder, and sea salt. Toss to coat the radishes well.

3. Place the radishes on the baking sheet and bake for 20 to 25 minutes, or until they are golden and fork-tender.

MASHED CAULIFLOWER
AND POTATOES

GLUTEN-FREE | NUT-FREE OPTION | OIL-FREE | SOY-FREE

SERVES 4 | PREP TIME: 10 minutes | COOK TIME: 15 minutes

Once again, cauliflower is sneaking into a recipe where you might not expect it—this time it's taking the place of a potato or two in mashed potatoes. I never peel my potatoes when making dishes like this because the peels have more nutrients than the flesh, including vitamins B and C, iron, and potassium. And it's much easier to leave the peels intact, cutting down on prep time. I like my potatoes on the lumpy side, so I don't spend too much time mashing them, but if you'd prefer them smoother, mash away until they reach the desired consistency.

2 large russet (or Yukon Gold)
   potatoes, chopped

3 cups chopped cauliflower florets

3 garlic cloves

Water

Sea salt

¼ cup plain, unsweetened nondairy milk
   (such as soy or almond)

¼ cup Homemade Vegetable Stock
   (page 20), or store-bought vegetable stock

Black pepper

Substitution tip: If you'd like to eliminate the potatoes from this recipe altogether, replace them with 6 more cups of cauliflower and eliminate the Homemade Vegetable Stock from the recipe.

Per serving: Calories: 172; Total fat: 1g; Total carbs: 37g; Fiber: 6g; Sugar: 3g; Protein: 6g; Sodium: 66mg

1. Place the potatoes, cauliflower florets, and garlic in a large stockpot with enough water to cover them plus two inches. Add 1/2 teaspoon of sea salt to the water and bring the pot to a boil over medium-high heat. Reduce the heat to medium-low and simmer for about 15 minutes, or until the vegetables are fork-tender.

2. Drain the vegetables, and then return them to the pot. Use a potato masher or large fork to mash the vegetables. Add the nondairy milk and Homemade Vegetable Stock and mash a little more, stirring as you go. Season with sea salt and black pepper to taste.

SCALLOPED SWEET POTATOES

GLUTEN-FREE | LOW-CARB | SOY-FREE

SERVES 8 | PREP TIME: 10 minutes | COOK TIME: 30 minutes

This recipe actually falls somewhere between scalloped potatoes and potatoes au gratin. Scalloped potatoes are usually made with a creamy sauce, whereas potatoes au gratin are made with a cheese sauce. "Gratin" comes from the French word for "grated." By definition, potatoes au gratin should be topped with grated bread crumbs, which I've left out here. Whatever you want to call it, this dish is warm and comforting.

2 pounds sweet potatoes, sliced thin (about ¼-inch thick), divided

1 teaspoon garlic powder, divided

1 teaspoon sea salt, divided

1 teaspoon black pepper, divided

2 cups Cheesy Vegetable Sauce (see page 24), divided

Prep tip: Slicing sweet potatoes by hand can be tricky, but it can be done. If you have a food processor with a slicing attachment, it can slice your sweet potatoes in a matter of minutes. A mandoline slicer can also be used.

Per serving: Calories: 159; Total fat: 0g; Total carbs: 28g; Fiber: 6g; Sugar: 6g; Protein: 6g; Sodium: 382mg

1. Preheat your oven to 425°F and lightly oil a 9-by-13-inch casserole or baking dish.

2. Layer half of the sliced sweet potatoes into the casserole dish. Sprinkle them with half the garlic powder, sea salt, and black pepper. The potatoes will overlap each other a little. Top with half of the Cheesy Vegetable Sauce. Layer on the rest of the sweet potato slices, and sprinkle them with the rest of the garlic powder, sea salt, and black pepper. Top everything with the remaining sauce.

3. Cover the dish with foil and bake for 30 minutes. Remove the foil and bake for another 10 minutes, or until the sweet potatoes are tender and the sauce is bubbly.

Kung Pao Brussels Sprouts, 114

CHAPTER EIGHT

DINNER MAINS

CRISPY ARTICHOKE TACOS

GLUTEN-FREE OPTION | NUT-FREE OPTION | OIL-FREE | SOY-FREE OPTION

MAKES 6 tacos | PREP TIME: 10 minutes | COOK TIME: 30 minutes

I've had people ask me what I use to make vegan tacos, and my answer is usually, "Anything I can get my hands on!" These tacos were inspired by fish tacos, and I've used battered artichoke hearts as the filling. Artichokes are low in calories and high in nutrients—including vitamins A, E, and K—and they're easy on the digestive system.

½ cup nondairy milk (such as soy or almond)

1 tablespoon cornstarch (or arrowroot)

½ cup cornmeal

1 teaspoon chili powder

½ teaspoon garlic powder

½ teaspoon sea salt

1 (14-ounce) can artichoke hearts, drained, patted dry, and quartered

2 cups thinly sliced red cabbage

2 cups thinly sliced green cabbage

2 carrots, grated or shredded

2 tablespoons lime juice

6 small (6- or 8-inch) whole-wheat or corn tortillas (or gluten-free tortillas), warmed

1 avocado, peeled, pitted, and sliced

1. Preheat your oven to 400°F and line a baking sheet with parchment paper.

2. In a medium bowl, whisk together the nondairy milk and cornstarch. In another medium bowl, mix together the cornmeal, chili powder, garlic powder, and sea salt.

3. Place the artichokes in the bowl with the nondairy milk mixture and toss to coat them well. Then, place them in the bowl with the cornmeal mixture and toss to coat them well.

4. Place the artichokes on the prepared baking sheet and bake them for about 30 minutes, or until crisp and golden brown, flipping them at the halfway point.

5. While the artichokes are cooking, mix together the red cabbage, green cabbage, carrots, and lime juice in a large bowl.

6. To assemble the tacos, place a few artichoke pieces in a tortilla and top with the cabbage mixture and avocado slices.

Substitution tip: Large romaine lettuce leaves can be used instead of tortillas.

Per serving: Calories: 202; Total fat: 6g; Total carbs: 36g; Fiber: 10g; Sugar: 4g; Protein: 6g; Sodium: 264mg

PORTOBELLO FAJITAS

GLUTEN-FREE OPTION | NUT-FREE | OIL-FREE OPTION | SOY-FREE

SERVES 4 | PREP TIME: 10 minutes | COOK TIME: 15 minutes

Vegetable fajitas are always a fun dish to order when eating out because all of the components are brought out individually and can be self-assembled into fajitas at the table. You can serve this dish that way, or you can put them together in the kitchen and serve them assembled. Top your fajitas with sliced avocados, diced tomatoes, chopped lettuce, and sliced jalapeño peppers, or with your favorite toppings.

1 teaspoon neutral-flavored oil (such as grapeseed or avocado)

1 medium red onion, halved and thinly sliced

4 large portobello mushrooms, sliced

3 bell peppers, seeded and thinly sliced

2 cloves garlic, minced

½ teaspoon chili powder

¼ teaspoon garlic powder

¼ teaspoon onion powder

¼ teaspoon sea salt

8 small (6- or 8-inch) whole-wheat or corn tortillas (or gluten-free tortillas), warmed

Substitution tip: Collard leaves can be used instead of tortillas. Also, try using my Homemade Vegetable Stock (see page 20) or water in place of the neutral-flavored oil.

Per serving: Calories: 354; Total fat: 10g; Total carbs: 59g; Fiber: 13g; Sugar: 10g; Protein: 14g; Sodium: 544mg

1. Heat the oil in a large sauté pan or cast-iron pan over medium-high heat. Add the onion and cook for about 5 minutes, until it begins to brown.

2. Add the portobello mushrooms, bell peppers, and garlic to the pan along with the chili powder, garlic powder, onion powder, and sea salt. Stir to coat the vegetables in the spices. Cook, stirring often, for about 10 minutes, or until the peppers have softened.

3. Assemble the fajitas by topping each tortilla with the portobello and pepper mixture. Top with your favorite toppings.

CHICKPEA CACCIATORE

GLUTEN-FREE | NUT-FREE | OIL-FREE OPTION | SOY-FREE

SERVES 4 | PREP TIME: **15 minutes** | COOK TIME: **25 minutes**

Cacciatore means "hunter" in Italian, and a cacciatore dish refers to food prepared "hunter-style" with herbs, tomatoes, and bell peppers. I don't think there's anything to hunt down in this vegan version, as chickpeas are readily available in just about any grocery store. Chickpeas are high in protein, fiber, folic acid, iron, magnesium, and zinc. You can serve this dish as is or over whole grain pasta or my Zucchini Noodles (see page 21).

1 teaspoon neutral-flavored oil (such as grapeseed or avocado)

½ onion, diced

2 garlic cloves, minced

1 red bell pepper, chopped

1 green bell pepper, chopped

8 ounces cremini mushrooms (or white button mushrooms), chopped

1 (28-ounce) can crushed tomatoes

1 (15-ounce) can chickpeas, drained and rinsed

1 teaspoon dried oregano

1 teaspoon dried thyme

1 teaspoon dried basil

Sea salt

Black pepper

Slow it down: This recipe can also be cooked in a slow cooker. Combine the ingredients in your slow cooker and cook on low for 8 hours.

Per serving: Calories: 227; Total fat: 3g; Total carbs: 40g; Fiber: 13g; Sugar: 18g; Protein: 13g; Sodium: 391mg

1. Heat the oil in a large sauté pan or cast-iron pan over medium-high heat. Add the onion and cook for about 5 minutes, until it has softened and begun to brown slightly.

2. Add the garlic, bell peppers, and mushrooms to the pan and cook, stirring frequently, for about 10 minutes, until the vegetables soften.

3. Add the crushed tomatoes, chickpeas, oregano, thyme, and basil to the pan and stir to combine everything. Bring the mixture to a boil, and then lower the heat to medium, cover the pan, and let simmer for about 10 minutes. Season with sea salt and black pepper to taste.

KUNG PAO BRUSSELS SPROUTS

GLUTEN-FREE OPTION | LOW-CARB | OIL-FREE OPTION

SERVES 4 | PREP TIME: 10 minutes | COOK TIME: 15 minutes

I like my stir-fries on the spicy side, and kung pao is one of my favorites. Here, I've used Brussels sprouts as the star of the dish. I've blanched them to make them tender, so they'll cook quicker in the stir-fry. If you'd like to add a little protein to this recipe, throw in some cubed Baked Tofu (see page 28). This dish can be served as is or with cooked brown rice or my Cauliflower Rice (see page 22).

1 pound Brussels sprouts, trimmed and halved

1 teaspoon neutral-flavored oil (such as grapeseed or avocado)

10 ounces cremini mushrooms (or white button mushrooms), chopped

1 red bell pepper, chopped

2 tablespoons low-sodium tamari (or soy sauce)

1 tablespoon rice vinegar (or apple cider vinegar)

1½ tablespoons cornstarch (or arrowroot)

2 garlic cloves, minced

1 tablespoon minced fresh ginger

1 teaspoon red pepper flakes

2 scallions, thinly sliced

¼ cup chopped peanuts

1. Prepare a large bowl with ice water and bring a large pot of salted water to a boil. Add the Brussels sprouts to the boiling water and cook for about 3 minutes, or until they're bright green.

2. Remove the Brussels sprouts from the pot with a slotted spoon or a skimmer, and immediately transfer them to the ice water bowl. Let them sit in the ice water for a minute. Remove the Brussels sprouts from the water and pat them dry with a towel.

3. Heat the oil in a large wok or sauté pan over medium-high heat. Add the mushrooms, bell pepper, and Brussels sprouts. Cook, stirring frequently, for about 10 minutes, or until the vegetables are tender.

4. In a small bowl, whisk together the tamari, rice vinegar, cornstarch, garlic, ginger, red pepper flakes, scallions, and peanuts. Pour the mixture into the pan, stirring to coat all the vegetables.

5. Cook, stirring frequently, for about 5 more minutes, or until the sauce has thickened and is heated throughout.

Substitution tip: Broccoli or cauliflower can be used in the place of Brussels sprouts. Also, try using my Homemade Vegetable Stock (see page 20) or water in place of the neutral-flavored oil.

Per serving: Calories: 151; Total fat: 5g; Total carbs: 21g; Fiber: 7g; Sugar: 6g; Protein: 10g; Sodium: 237mg

EGGPLANT MARSALA

GLUTEN-FREE OPTION | LOW-CARB | NUT-FREE | OIL-FREE OPTION

SERVES 4 | PREP TIME: 10 minutes | COOK TIME: 20 minutes

Don't peel those eggplants! I like to cook the eggplant in its skin because it's loaded with the compound nasunin, which has many health benefits, including protecting cells from damage, lowering cholesterol, preventing neuroinflammation, and facilitating blood flow to the brain. Eggplants are also rich in B vitamins, potassium, magnesium, and folic acid. This dish can be served as is or over my Cauliflower Rice (see page 22) or Mashed Cauliflower and Potatoes (see page 106).

2 tablespoons balsamic vinegar

2 tablespoons low-sodium tamari (or soy sauce)

1 tablespoon neutral-flavored oil (such as grapeseed or avocado), plus one teaspoon

2 large eggplants, ends trimmed, sliced lengthwise (about ½-inch thick)

1½ pounds cremini mushrooms (or white button mushrooms), sliced

2 garlic cloves, minced

½ teaspoon sea salt

½ teaspoon dried thyme

2 cups marsala wine

1 cup Homemade Vegetable Stock (see page 20), or store-bought vegetable stock

2 tablespoons chopped parsley

1. Preheat your oven to 400°F and line a baking sheet with parchment paper.

2. In a small bowl, whisk together the balsamic vinegar, tamari, and 1 tablespoon of oil.

3. Place the eggplant slices on the baking sheet and brush both sides with the vinegar mixture. Bake the slices for 10 minutes, flip them and bake for another 10 minutes.

4. While the eggplant is baking, cook the mushrooms. Heat the remaining oil in a large sauté pan or cast-iron pan over medium-high heat. Add the mushrooms and cook, stirring often, for about 10 minutes, until they begin to brown.

5. Add the garlic, salt, thyme, wine, and Homemade Vegetable Stock to the pan. Bring to a boil, then reduce the heat to medium-low, cover the pan, and let the mixture simmer for about 10 minutes, or until the mixture has reduced by half.

6. Divide the eggplant slices among 4 plates and top them with the mushroom mixture and parsley.

Substitution tip: My Cauliflower Steaks (see page 118) can be used instead of eggplant. Also, try using my Homemade Vegetable Stock or water in place of the neutral-flavored oil.

Per serving: Calories: 217; Total fat: 2g; Total carbs: 27g; Fiber: 12g; Sugar: 13g; Protein: 9g; Sodium: 348mg

CAULIFLOWER STEAKS WITH SPINACH PESTO

GLUTEN-FREE | LOW-CARB | NUT-FREE | OIL-FREE OPTION | SOY-FREE

SERVES 2 | PREP TIME: 10 minutes | COOK TIME: 30 minutes

I like to show people how to make cauliflower steaks in my cooking classes because it's one of those dishes that looks daunting but is actually super-easy to make. Since it looks pretty on a plate, it's a terrific dish for date night or a dinner party, but it's simple enough to make for weeknights, when there often is not a great deal of time available for food prep and cooking. I like to serve this dish with my Mashed Cauliflower and Potatoes (see page 106) and Black Pepper Mushrooms (see page 101).

FOR THE CAULIFLOWER:

1 large cauliflower head, leaves and stem trimmed (do not core the cauliflower)
1 tablespoon neutral-flavored oil (such as grapeseed or avocado)
½ teaspoon sea salt
½ teaspoon black pepper

FOR THE SPINACH PESTO:

2 cups fresh baby spinach, packed
½ cup fresh basil, packed
1 tablespoon pine nuts
1 garlic clove, minced
2 teaspoons lemon juice
½ teaspoon sea salt
2 tablespoons extra-virgin olive oil

1. Preheat your oven to 400°F and line a baking sheet with parchment paper.

2. With the cauliflower sitting on its stem, slice it into large slabs, about 1-inch thick. Slice it the same way you would slice a loaf of bread. You should end up with 3 or 4 large slabs. Place them on the prepared baking sheet.

3. Brush both sides of the cauliflower steaks with the oil, and then sprinkle them with the sea salt and black pepper. Roast the slabs for 25 to 30 minutes, or until golden brown, carefully flipping them at halfway point.

4. While the cauliflower is roasting, make the spinach pesto. Place the spinach, basil, pine nuts, garlic, lemon juice, and sea salt in a food processor and process until the ingredients are coarsely chopped. While the processor is still running, add the olive oil through the top opening. Process the pesto until it's thoroughly mixed but not a paste.

5. Drizzle the spinach pesto over the cauliflower steaks.

Make-ahead tip: The pesto can be made ahead of time and stored in the refrigerator. Pesto can also be premade and frozen.

Substitution tip: Try using my Homemade Vegetable Stock (see page 20) or water in place of the neutral-flavored oil.

Per serving: Calories: 267; Total fat: 18g; Total carbs: 25g; Fiber: 12g; Sugar: 11g; Protein: 10g; Sodium: 620mg

TOMATO AND ARUGULA PIZZA WITH CAULIFLOWER CRUST

GLUTEN-FREE OPTION | OIL-FREE | SOY-FREE

MAKES 1 (12-inch) pizza | PREP TIME: 15 minutes, plus cashew soaking time | COOK TIME: 25 minutes

Cauliflower pizza crust may look daunting, but it's surprisingly easy to make. Chia seeds and flaxseed can be a little tricky to find, but they're essential in this recipe for binding the dough mixture together. Most grocery stores keep them in the supplement or natural foods area. In addition to acting as a binder, they're also loaded with omega-3 fatty acids and fiber.

1 batch Cauliflower Rice (see page 22), cooked

½ cup whole-wheat flour (or all-purpose gluten-free flour mix)

¼ cup cornstarch (or arrowroot)

¼ cup chia seeds (or ground flaxseeds)

1 teaspoon garlic powder

1 teaspoon sea salt, divided

½ cup raw cashews, soaked for two hours, rinsed, and drained

3 tablespoons water, plus more if needed

1 tablespoon lemon juice

1 tablespoon nutritional yeast

1 garlic clove, minced

1 cup Quick and Easy Tomato Sauce (see page 27) or store-bought tomato sauce

2½ ounces arugula, chopped

2 large tomatoes, chopped

1 (14-ounce) can artichoke hearts, drained and quartered

½ teaspoon red pepper flakes, optional

1. Preheat your oven to 450°F.

2. Place the cauliflower rice in a large bowl along with the flour, cornstarch, chia seeds, garlic powder, and ½ teaspoon sea salt. Mix everything together, kneading with your hands to help it stick together. Form a ball with the dough.

3. Place the dough on a piece of parchment paper and place a second piece of parchment paper on top of it. Use a rolling pin to form the ball into a large, smooth circle, about 1/4-inch thick. Remove the top piece of parchment paper, and carefully lift the crust using the bottom piece of parchment paper. Place the crust on a baking sheet. If you don't have a rolling pin, place a piece of parchment paper on a baking sheet and use your hands to press and shape the dough.

4. Bake the crust for 18 to 20 minutes, or until the edges have browned.

5. While the crust is baking, make the cashew cheese. Place the cashews, water, lemon juice, nutritional yeast, garlic, and ½ teaspoon sea salt in a blender or food processer. Process until smooth and creamy. If the mixture is too thick, add more water, 1 teaspoon at a time.

6. After removing the crust from the oven, carefully flip the crust over. Do this by placing a new piece of parchment paper on top of the crust while it is still on the baking sheet. Hold a large cutting board over the top of the newly placed parchment paper, and flip the baking sheet upside-down, using the cutting board as support for the crust. Then peel off the original piece of parchment paper that the crust was baking on.

7. Spread the Quick and Easy Tomato Sauce over the crust, top with the arugula, tomatoes, artichoke hearts, and red pepper flakes (if using). Drizzle with the cashew cheese.

8. Slide the pizza back onto a baking sheet and bake for an additional 5 minutes, or until the toppings have heated throughout.

Make-ahead tip: The crust and cashew cheese can both be made ahead of time and stored in the refrigerator until you're ready to assemble your pizza.

Per serving (1/4 pizza): Calories: 377; Total fat: 12g; Total carbs: 56g; Fiber: 17g; Sugar: 9g; Protein: 17g; Sodium: 732mg

ZUCCHINI AND RED PEPPER ENCHILADAS

GLUTEN-FREE OPTION | NUT-FREE | OIL-FREE OPTION | SOY-FREE

SERVES 4 | PREP TIME: 15 minutes | COOK TIME: 35 minutes

I've cheated a little with this dish as I've taken a shortcut with the sauce. Most enchilada sauce recipes are time consuming and require a bunch of ingredients. I've simply taken my Quick and Easy Tomato Sauce and added a few spices. I like to serve these enchiladas topped with my Cheesy Vegetable Sauce, diced avocado, and fresh jalapeño slices.

1 teaspoon neutral-flavored oil (such as grapeseed or avocado)

1 small onion, diced

1 garlic clove, minced

1 red bell pepper, chopped

1 large zucchini, chopped

1 (15-ounce) can black beans, drained and rinsed

2 cups Quick and Easy Tomato Sauce (see page 27), or store-bought tomato sauce

2 teaspoons chili powder

1 teaspoon garlic powder

½ teaspoon red pepper flakes

8 large (10- to -12-inch) whole-wheat or corn tortillas (or gluten-free tortillas)

½ cup Cheesy Vegetable Sauce (see page 24), optional

1. Preheat your oven to 350°F and have a 9-by-13-inch casserole or baking dish ready.

2. Heat the oil in a large sauté pan or cast-iron pan over medium-high heat. Add the onion and cook for about 5 minutes, until it has softened and begun to brown slightly.

3. Add the garlic, bell pepper, and zucchini and continue cooking for about 10 minutes, until the vegetables have softened. Remove from heat and stir in the black beans.

4. In a medium-size bowl, mix together the Quick and Easy Tomato Sauce with the chili powder, garlic powder, and red pepper flakes. Spoon half of it onto the bottom of your casserole dish.

5. Assemble the enchiladas by placing about ½ cup of the mixture onto the center of a tortilla. Carefully roll the tortilla up and place it seam-side down in the casserole dish. Repeat with the remaining tortillas and filling. Pour the rest of the sauce over the enchiladas, cover the dish with foil, and bake for 20 minutes.

6. Drizzle with the Cheesy Vegetable Sauce (if using).

Make-ahead tip: The vegetables can be cooked ahead of time and stored in the refrigerator until you're ready to assemble the enchiladas.

Substitution tip: Try using my Homemade Vegetable Stock (see page 20) or water in place of the neutral-flavored oil.

Per serving: Calories: 620; Total fat: 11g; Total carbs: 110g; Fiber: 15g; Sugar: 9g; Protein: 22g; Sodium: 721mg

CHICKPEA POT PIE

GLUTEN-FREE OPTION | NUT-FREE | SOY-FREE

SERVES 6 | PREP TIME: 20 minutes | COOK TIME: 60 minutes

This recipe may look a little daunting, but trust me—it's easy to put together. The dough for the crust comes together quickly, as do the vegetables used for the filling. Most of the cooking time is inactive, so this is a great recipe to assemble when you get home from work, pop it in the oven, and then put your feet up while it cooks.

FOR THE CRUST:

1¼ cups whole-wheat flour (or all-purpose gluten-free flour mix)

1 teaspoon sea salt

⅓ cup ice-cold olive oil

⅓ cup ice water

FOR THE FILLING:

1 teaspoon neutral-flavored oil (such as grapeseed or avocado)

1 medium onion, diced

2 garlic cloves, minced

1 small sweet potato, diced

1 carrot, chopped

5 ounces cremini mushrooms (or white button mushrooms), chopped

½ cup peas, fresh or frozen and thawed

1 (15-ounce) can chickpeas, drained and rinsed

¼ cup whole-wheat (or gluten-free) flour

1¼ cups Homemade Vegetable Stock (see page 20), or store-bought vegetable stock

½ teaspoon sea salt

½ teaspoon black pepper

1. To make the crust: Mix together the whole-wheat flour and sea salt in a large bowl. Drizzle the olive oil over the mixture. Use a rubber spatula or wooden spoon to mix everything together until the flour resembles pebbles. Don't break up the lumps.

2. Drizzle the ice water over the mixture, mixing as you go until it forms a dough. You may need to knead it a little with your hands. Don't over-knead the mixture. Form the dough into a ball, wrap it in plastic wrap, and place it in the refrigerator while you cook the filling.

3. Preheat your oven to 350°F and have a 9-inch pie pan ready. If you don't have a pie pan, you can use a small baking dish.

4. To make the filling: Heat the oil in a large sauté pan or cast-iron pan over medium-high heat. Add the onion and cook for about 5 minutes, until it has softened and begun to brown slightly. Add the garlic, sweet potato, carrots, and mushrooms to the pan and continue to cook, stirring frequently, for 10 minutes, or until the vegetables have softened. Add the peas and chickpeas to the pan and stir to combine.

5. Sprinkle the vegetables with the flour, and then add the Homemade Vegetable Stock, sea salt, and black pepper, and stir to combine everything. Cook, stirring frequently, for 5 more minutes, or until the mixture thickens. Pour the mixture into the pie pan.

6. Place the dough on a medium-size piece of parchment paper and cover with another piece of parchment paper. Use a rolling pin to roll the dough from the center out until it forms a 9-inch circle. Carefully place the dough on top of the pie pan and trim any excess that's hanging over the edge. Crimp the edges of the pie crust by pinching it with your fingers or pressing it down with a fork. Bake for 35 to 40 minutes, or until the crust is golden brown.

Ingredient tip: Place your oil in the freezer about 1 hour before you're going to make the pie crust so that it thickens.

Substitution tip: Try using my Homemade Vegetable Stock or water in place of the neutral-flavored oil when sautéing the vegetables.

Per serving: Calories: 362; Total fat: 17g; Total carbs: 46g; Fiber: 6g; Sugar: 5g; Protein: 9g; Sodium: 284mg

SHEPHERDESS'S PIE WITH SWEET POTATO CRUST

GLUTEN-FREE | NUT-FREE | SOY-FREE

SERVES 6 | PREP TIME: 10 minutes | COOK TIME: 30 minutes

Shepherd's pie is traditionally made with lamb (the similar cottage pie is made with beef), so I like to refer to the meat-free version as Shepherdess's Pie. I've used hearty lentils in this dish since they have a meaty texture. Shepherd's pie is also typically topped with mashed potatoes, but I've used sweet potatoes in this recipe because they're loaded with beta-carotene and lycopene, which are known to support eye health.

4 sweet potatoes, diced

Water

Sea salt

1 teaspoon neutral-flavored oil (such as grapeseed or avocado)

1 medium onion, diced

2 garlic cloves, minced

2 carrots, chopped

8 ounces cremini mushrooms (or white button mushrooms), chopped

2 (15-ounce) cans brown lentils, drained and rinsed

1 (15-ounce) can diced tomatoes, drained

2 tablespoons tomato paste

1 teaspoon dried thyme

¼ cup Homemade Vegetable Stock (see page 20) or store-bought vegetable stock

Black pepper

1. Preheat your oven to 400°F and have a 9-by-13-inch casserole or baking dish ready.

2. Place the sweet potatoes in a large stockpot with enough water to cover them plus two inches. Add a pinch of sea salt to the water and bring the pot to a boil over medium-high heat. Reduce the heat to medium-low and simmer for about 15 minutes, or until the sweet potatoes are fork-tender.

3. While the sweet potatoes are cooking, prepare the filling. Heat the oil in a large sauté pan or cast-iron pan over medium-high heat. Add the onion and cook for about 5 minutes, until it has softened and begun to brown slightly. Add the garlic, carrots, and mushrooms to the pan and continue to cook, stirring frequently, for about 10 minutes, or until the vegetables have softened.

4. Mix in the lentils, diced tomatoes, tomato paste, and thyme. Remove the pan from the heat and pour the mixture into the 9-by-13-inch casserole dish.

5. Drain the sweet potatoes and then return them to the pot. Use a potato masher or large fork to mash the vegetables. Add the Homemade Vegetable Stock and mash a little more. Season with sea salt and black pepper to taste.

6. Carefully spread the mashed sweet potatoes over the top of the lentil mixture. Bake for about 15 minutes, or until the sweet potato crust has browned slightly and the filling is bubbly.

Substitution tip: Mashed Cauliflower and Potatoes (see page 106) can be used as the crust instead of sweet potatoes. Also, try using my Homemade Vegetable Stock or water in place of the neutral-flavored oil.

Per serving: Calories: 255; Total fat: 2g; Total carbs: 49g; Fiber: 14g; Sugar: 11g; Protein: 14g; Sodium: 134mg

Vegetable Lasagna, 136

PASTAS, NOODLES, AND RICE

COLD SESAME NOODLES

GLUTEN-FREE OPTION | LOW-CARB | NUT-FREE | OIL-FREE

SERVES 4 | PREP TIME: 10 minutes

This is a great idea for hot summer days, when it's too hot to cook. It's a versatile dish, too, so you can customize the vegetables in the recipe to your liking. I've used cucumbers and carrots here, but I sometimes like to make it with sliced red pepper and blanched broccoli. If you'd prefer, my cubed Baked Tofu (see page 28) can also be added to it.

¼ cup tahini

3 tablespoons rice vinegar (or apple cider vinegar)

3 tablespoons low-sodium tamari (or soy sauce)

1 teaspoon maple syrup (or agave)

2 teaspoons fresh grated ginger

1 garlic clove, minded

1 teaspoon red pepper flakes

Water

1 batch Zucchini Noodles (see page 21)

1 medium cucumber, thinly sliced

1 medium carrot, grated or shredded

2 scallions, chopped

2 tablespoons sesame seeds

¼ cup chopped cilantro

Substitution tip: Cooked udon, soba, or rice noodles can be used in the place of Zucchini Noodles.

1. In a small bowl, whisk together the tahini, rice vinegar, tamari, maple syrup, ginger, garlic, and red pepper flakes. If the mixture seems too thick, add water, 1 tablespoon at a time.

2. Place the Zucchini Noodles in a large bowl, pour the dressing over the noodles, and gently toss to coat them well. Add the cucumber, carrot, and scallions to the bowl and gently fold them into the noodles. Top with sesame seeds and cilantro.

Per serving: Calories: 176; Total fat: 11g; Total carbs: 16g; Fiber: 4g; Sugar: 5g; Protein: 6g; Sodium: 392mg

PAD THAI

GLUTEN-FREE OPTION | OIL-FREE OPTION

SERVES 4 | PREP TIME: **10 minutes** | COOK TIME: **15 minutes**

Pad Thai is a favorite of mine, but it's a tricky dish to order out in restaurants because eggs are often added to it. I like to make it at home to ensure that it's vegan and so I can add extra vegetables. In this recipe, I've used broccoli, baby bok choy, and mushrooms, but it can be customized to use whatever veggies you have on hand. Cabbage, red peppers, and scallions are wonderful additions.

8 ounces rice noodles

¼ cup low-sodium tamari (or soy sauce)

2 tablespoons rice vinegar (or apple cider vinegar)

2 tablespoons lime juice

2 tablespoons agave (or maple) syrup

2 garlic cloves, minced

1 teaspoon neutral-flavored oil (such as grapeseed or avocado)

4 cups chopped broccoli florets

4 cups chopped baby bok choy

2 cups shiitake mushrooms, sliced

16 ounces Baked Tofu (see page 28) or store-bought baked tofu

1 cup mung bean sprouts

¼ cup chopped peanuts

Substitution tip: Zucchini Noodles (see page 21) can be used instead of rice noodles. Also, try using my Homemade Vegetable Stock (see page 20) or water in place of the neutral-flavored oil.

Per serving: Calories: 476; Total fat: 10g; Total carbs: 80g; Fiber: 8g; Sugar: 13g; Protein: 21g; Sodium: 789mg

1. Cook the rice noodles according to the package instructions.

2. In a small bowl, whisk together the tamari, rice vinegar, lime juice, agave, and garlic.

3. Heat the oil in a large wok or sauté pan over medium-high heat. Add the broccoli, bok choy, and mushrooms, and cook, stirring frequently, for about 10 minutes, until the vegetables have softened.

4. Add the noodles, baked tofu, and sauce to the pan, and cook, stirring frequently, until all of the sauce has been absorbed and everything is heated throughout.

5. Serve topped with mung bean sprouts and chopped peanuts.

PASTA PRIMAVERA

GLUTEN-FREE OPTION | NUT-FREE | OIL-FREE | SOY-FREE

SERVES 6 | PREP TIME: 10 minutes | COOK TIME: 10 minutes

Boiling vegetables in the water with the pasta is a trick I learned several years ago. It saves both cooking and clean-up time. It works well with vegetables like broccoli, asparagus, green beans, and cauliflower. Simply add the chopped vegetables to the pot with the pasta about five minutes before the pasta is done, and the vegetables cook alongside the pasta. When the pasta is ready, just drain the contents of the pot as you usually would.

8 quarts water

12 ounces whole grain (or gluten-free) pasta

4 cups chopped broccoli florets

1 pound asparagus, tough ends removed, chopped

½ cup peas, fresh or frozen and thawed

4 cups Creamy Cauliflower Sauce (see page 23)

1 cup cherry tomatoes, sliced in half

Sea salt

Black pepper

1 cup chopped parsley

Substitution tip: Cauliflower and green beans can be used in the place of broccoli and asparagus.

Per serving: Calories: 297; Total fat: 2g; Total carbs: 60g; Fiber: 8g; Sugar: 8g; Protein: 11g; Sodium: 301mg

1. Heat 8 quarts of water in a large stockpot over medium-high heat and bring to a boil. Add the pasta and cook according to the package instructions. About 5 minutes before the pasta is done, add the broccoli, asparagus, and peas. Drain the pasta and vegetables and return them to the pot.

2. Add the Creamy Cauliflower Sauce to the pot and stir gently to combine everything. Stir in the cherry tomatoes. Season with sea salt and black pepper to taste. Top with the chopped parsley.

MAC AND "CHEESE" WITH BROCCOLI

GLUTEN-FREE OPTION | OIL-FREE | SOY-FREE

SERVES 6 | PREP TIME: 5 minutes | COOK TIME: 10 minutes

I doubt there's a more comforting dish than macaroni and cheese. I like to add broccoli to my mac and cheese because not only do the little florets pick up lots of the cheesy sauce, making them extra delicious, but broccoli is also highly nutritious. In fact, it's one of the most nutrient-dense foods on the planet. It's a good source of protein (yes, protein!), as well as vitamins A, C, and K; folic acid; potassium; and magnesium.

8 quarts water

12 ounces bite-size whole grain (or gluten-free) pasta

4 cups chopped broccoli florets

4 cups Cheesy Vegetable Sauce (see page 24)

Sea salt

Black pepper

Slow it down: If you'd like to make a mac and cheese casserole-style dish, cook the pasta *al dente*, so that it's not quite done. Preheat your oven to 400°F. After step 2, pour the mac and cheese into a 9-by-13-inch casserole or baking dish, sprinkle on half a cup of whole-wheat or gluten-free panko bread crumbs, and bake for about 20 minutes, or until the bread crumbs are golden brown.

Per serving: Calories: 421; Total fat: 2g; Total carbs: 65g; Fiber: 8g; Sugar: 4g; Protein: 18g; Sodium: 310mg

1. Heat the water in a large stockpot over medium-high heat and bring to a boil. Add the pasta and cook according to the package instructions. About 5 minutes before the pasta is done, add the broccoli. Drain the pasta and broccoli and return them to the pot.

2. Add the Cheesy Vegetable Sauce to the pot and stir gently to combine everything. Season with sea salt and black pepper to taste.

CREAMY MUSHROOM STROGANOFF

GLUTEN-FREE OPTION | NUT-FREE | OIL-FREE OPTION | SOY-FREE

SERVES 6 | PREP TIME: 10 minutes | COOK TIME: 15 minutes

Stroganoff is traditionally made with beef and mushrooms in a cream sauce, but the mushrooms are the star of this vegan version. I like to make this recipe with white button or cremini mushrooms (which are sometimes also called baby bellas), which are both excellent sources of selenium, potassium, and zinc, as well as thiamine, riboflavin, and niacin. Creminis are also high in B vitamins.

6 quarts water

12 ounces whole grain (or gluten-free) pasta

1 teaspoon neutral-flavored oil (such as grapeseed or avocado)

1 small onion, diced

3 garlic cloves, minced

20 ounces cremini mushrooms (or white button mushrooms), sliced

4 cups Creamy Cauliflower Sauce (see page 23)

Sea salt

Black pepper

¼ cup chopped parsley

Substitution tip: Zucchini Noodles (see page 21) can be used in the place of pasta. This dish can also be served over cooked brown rice or my Cauliflower Rice (see page 22). Also, try using my Homemade Vegetable Stock (see page 20) or water in place of the neutral-flavored oil.

Per serving: Calories: 285; Total fat: 3g; Total carbs: 56g; Fiber: 5g; Sugar: 6g; Protein: 10g; Sodium: 286mg

1. Heat 6 quarts of water in a large stockpot over medium-high heat and bring it to a boil. Add the pasta and cook according to the package instructions. Drain the pasta and return it to the pot.

2. While the pasta is boiling, cook the vegetables. Heat the oil in a large sauté pan or cast-iron pan over medium-high heat. Add the onion and cook for about 5 minutes, until it has softened and begun to brown slightly. Add the garlic and cook for another 1 to 2 minutes. Add the mushrooms and cook for 10 minutes, stirring frequently, until the mushrooms have released their liquid and begun to brown.

3. Add the Creamy Cauliflower Sauce and cooked mushrooms to the pot with the pasta and gently stir to combine. Season with sea salt and black pepper to taste, and top with the chopped parsley.

PASTA BOLOGNESE

GLUTEN-FREE OPTION | OIL-FREE | SOY-FREE

SERVES 6 | PREP TIME: **5 minutes** | COOK TIME: **10 minutes**

Made with Quick and Easy Tomato Sauce and Hearty Veggie Crumbles, there are a lot of vegetables hidden in this dish, but no one will know unless you tell them. Bolognese is traditionally served over broad, flat pasta noodles, such as fettuccini or pappardelle, but it's delicious with any type of pasta. I sometimes like to add steamed greens, such as spinach or kale, for an extra boost of nutrition.

6 quarts water

12 ounces whole grain (or gluten-free) pasta

4 cups Quick and Easy Tomato Sauce (see page 27), or store-bought tomato sauce

2 cups Hearty Veggie Crumbles (see page 29)

Sea salt

Black pepper

Substitution tip: Zucchini Noodles (see page 21) can be used in the place of pasta.

Per serving: Calories: 273; Total fat: 2g; Total carbs: 54g; Fiber: 4g; Sugar: 7g; Protein: 11g; Sodium: 382mg

Heat 6 quarts of water in a large stockpot over medium-high heat and bring it to a boil. Add the pasta and cook according to the package instructions. Drain the pasta and return it to the pot. Add the Quick and Easy Tomato Sauce and Hearty Veggie Crumbles to the pot and gently stir to combine. Season with sea salt and black pepper to taste.

VEGETABLE LASAGNA

GLUTEN-FREE | LOW-CARB | NUT-FREE | OIL-FREE

SERVES 8 | PREP TIME: 15 minutes, plus salting time | COOK TIME: 45 minutes

Lasagna has always been my favorite meal. This healthy vegetable version is made using eggplant and zucchini instead of noodles. Eggplant and zucchini tend to be very watery, so salting them is necessary to remove some of the moisture. Salting also softens the vegetables, helping them cook quicker. I've skipped the salting step in the past, only to find that my zucchini and eggplant were still firm and almost raw, despite being baked in the lasagna for half an hour.

2 medium eggplants, ends trimmed, sliced lengthwise, ⅛-inch to ¼-inch thick

4 medium zucchinis, ends trimmed, sliced lengthwise, ⅛-inch to ¼-inch thick

Sea salt

1 (14-ounce) package extra-firm tofu, drained and pressed

¼ cup lemon juice

¼ cup nutritional yeast

2 garlic cloves, minced

1 teaspoon dried basil

½ teaspoon sea salt

5 ounces baby spinach

4 cups Quick and Easy Tomato Sauce (see page 27) or store-bought tomato sauce

1. Preheat your oven to 375°F and have a 9-by-13-inch casserole or baking dish ready.

2. Lay the zucchini and eggplant slices onto cooling racks or towels and sprinkle them with sea salt. Let them sit for 20 minutes. Pat the slices dry with a towel, flip them over, and sprinkle them with salt again. Let them sit for another 20 minutes. Rinse the pieces and then pat them dry.

3. Blend the tofu, lemon juice, nutritional yeast, garlic, basil, and sea salt together in a food processor until it's thick and looks like ricotta cheese. Add the spinach and pulse two or three times to incorporate it into the mixture. If you don't have a food processor, coarsely chop the spinach. Mash the tofu mixture together with a potato masher or large fork until all the large lumps are gone and fold the spinach into the mixture.

4. Spoon a thin layer of the Quick and Easy Tomato Sauce over the bottom of the casserole or baking dish. Layer on a third of the eggplant and zucchini slices and top with half of the tofu ricotta and 1/3 of the tomato sauce. Repeat with another layer of eggplant and zucchini slices, tofu ricotta, and tomato sauce. Top with the remaining eggplant and zucchini, and tomato sauce.

5. Cover the dish with foil and bake for 30 minutes. Remove the foil and bake for another 15 minutes, or until the sauce is hot and bubbly. Let the lasagna sit for 10 minutes before slicing and serving.

Prep tip: This recipe works best when the vegetables are sliced very thin. A mandoline slicer is handy for getting thin, uniform slices, but a sharp knife can be used as well.

Per serving: Calories: 151; Total fat: 3g; Total carbs: 23g; Fiber: 11g; Sugar: 12g; Protein: 13g; Sodium: 321mg

BUDDHA BOWL

GLUTEN-FREE | NUT-FREE OPTION | OIL-FREE OPTION

SERVES 4 | PREP TIME: 15 minutes | COOK TIME: 30 minutes

A Buddha Bowl is simply a bowl filled with cooked grains, a protein such as chickpeas or tofu, and vegetables. They're usually artfully arranged, with each component having its own place in the bowl, rather than all of the ingredients tossed together. The possibilities for my Buddha Bowls are endless, as pretty much any grain, plant-based protein, and vegetable can be used. Brown rice or cauliflower rice can be used in the place of quinoa, chickpeas or cooked tempeh can be used in the place of tofu, and your favorite veggies can be roasted instead of using cauliflower or Brussels sprouts.

1 medium head cauliflower, chopped into bite-size florets

16 ounces Brussels sprouts, trimmed and sliced in half

2 tablespoons neutral-flavored oil (such as grapeseed or avocado), divided

1 teaspoon sea salt, divided

½ teaspoon black pepper

1 cup quinoa, rinsed

2 cups Homemade Vegetable Stock (see page 20), or store-bought vegetable stock

4 cups chopped curly kale

16 ounces Baked Tofu (see page 28) or store-bought baked tofu

1 cup Tahini Dressing (see page 25) or Spicy Peanut Dressing (see page 26)

1. Preheat your oven to 400°F and line a baking sheet with parchment paper.

2. Place the cauliflower and Brussels sprouts in a large bowl along with 1 tablespoon of oil, ½ teaspoon of sea salt, and the black pepper. Toss everything to coat the vegetables well. Spread the vegetables out on the prepared baking sheet and bake them for 30 minutes, flipping them after 15 minutes.

3. While the vegetables are roasting, place the quinoa and Homemade Vegetable Stock in a medium saucepot and bring to a boil over medium-high heat. Reduce the heat to medium-low, cover the pot, and allow the quinoa to simmer for about 15 minutes, or until all the liquid has been absorbed.

4. Place the kale in a large bowl with the remaining oil and sea salt. Gently knead the kale until it begins to soften and wilt.

5. To assemble the bowls, divide the cooked quinoa among four bowls. Top with the roasted vegetables, massaged kale, and Baked Tofu. Drizzle with the dressing.

Make-ahead tip: All of the components can be made ahead of time and stored in the refrigerator. The bowls can be assembled at dinnertime. Buddha Bowls are just as delicious when served cold as they are when served hot.

Substitution tip: Try using my Homemade Vegetable Stock or water in place of the neutral-flavored oil.

Per serving: Calories: 587; Total fat: 31g; Total carbs: 60g; Fiber: 15g; Sugar: 7g; Protein: 28g; Sodium: 454mg

GARLICKY VEGETABLE FRIED RICE

GLUTEN-FREE OPTION | LOW-CARB | NUT-FREE | OIL-FREE OPTION

SERVES 4 | PREP TIME: **10 minutes** | COOK TIME: **17 minutes**

Vegetable fried rice is usually made at restaurants with carrots, peas, and corn and served as a side dish. I like to load my rice up with extra veggies and serve it as a main course for a quick dinner. In this recipe, I've used scallions, broccoli, bell pepper, carrot, and peas. Feel free to play with what you include. Mushrooms and snap peas would also be terrific additions.

1 teaspoon neutral-flavored oil (such as grapeseed or avocado)

4 garlic cloves, minced

2 teaspoons minced or grated fresh ginger

3 scallions, chopped

3 cups broccoli florets

1 red bell pepper, chopped

1 carrot, chopped

1 cup peas (or edamame), fresh or frozen and thawed

4 cups Cauliflower Rice (see page 22) or store-bought, uncooked

3 tablespoons low-sodium tamari (or soy sauce)

2 tablespoons rice vinegar (or apple cider vinegar)

¼ teaspoon red pepper flakes

Sea salt

Black pepper

1. Heat the oil in a large wok or sauté pan over medium-high heat. Add the garlic, ginger, and scallions, and cook for 1 to 2 minutes, stirring often. Add the broccoli, bell pepper, carrot, peas, and cauliflower rice to the pan and cook for 5 more minutes, stirring frequently.

2. Whisk together the tamari, vinegar, and red pepper flakes. Pour the mixture into the pan and stir to combine everything.

3. Cook for 10 more minutes, stirring frequently, until the vegetables are tender. Season with sea salt and black pepper to taste.

Substitution tip: Cooked brown rice can be used instead of Cauliflower Rice. If you are using brown rice, add it to the pan in step 2 rather than step 1.

Per serving: Calories: 117; Total fat: 1g; Total carbs: 23g; Fiber: 7g; Sugar: 8g; Protein: 8g; Sodium: 418mg

MUSHROOM PAELLA

GLUTEN-FREE | NUT-FREE | OIL-FREE OPTION | SOY-FREE

SERVES 6 | PREP TIME: **10 minutes** | COOK TIME: **22 minutes**

This recipe doesn't really resemble traditional paella, which is made with seafood and arborio rice, but I created it in the spirit of paella. Arborio rice is a starchy, short-grain white rice that cooks up to a creamy consistency. Brown arborio rice does exist, but it's difficult to find. Since white arborio isn't a whole grain, I've used regular brown rice in this recipe, and I've pre-cooked it to get dinner on the table quickly. Saffron threads traditionally give paella a yellowish hue, but it's pretty pricey, so I've cheated here and used turmeric in its place.

1 teaspoon neutral-flavored oil (such as grapeseed or avocado)

1 small onion, diced

3 garlic cloves, minced

16 ounces assorted mushrooms, chopped (See Ingredient tip)

1 red bell pepper, sliced

1 (14-ounce) can diced tomatoes with their juices

1 cup Homemade Vegetable Stock (see page 20) or store-bought vegetable stock

4 cups cooked brown rice

1 cup peas, fresh or frozen and thawed

1 teaspoon paprika

1 teaspoon turmeric

Sea salt

Black pepper

¼ cup chopped parsley

2 lemons, cut into wedges

1. Heat the oil in a large sauté pan over medium-high heat. Add the onion and cook for about 5 minutes, until it has softened and begun to brown slightly. Add the garlic and cook for another 1 to 2 minutes.

2. Add the mushrooms and red bell pepper and cook, stirring frequently, for about 10 minutes, until the vegetables soften. Add the diced tomatoes with their juices, Homemade Vegetable Stock, brown rice, peas, paprika, and turmeric to the pan and stir to combine everything. Bring the mixture to a boil and then lower the heat to medium, cover the pan, and allow the dish to simmer for about 5 minutes, or until most of the liquid has been absorbed.

CONTINUED

3. Season with sea salt and black pepper to taste, top with chopped parsley, and serve with lemon wedges.

Ingredient tip: For the assorted mushrooms, I like to use a mixture of cremini, shiitake, and oyster.

Substitution tip: My Cauliflower Rice (see page 22) can be used instead of brown rice. Try using my Homemade Vegetable Stock or water in place of the neutral-flavored oil.

Per serving: Calories: 198; Total fat: 2g; Total carbs: 39g; Fiber: 3g; Sugar: 5g; Protein: 7g; Sodium: 126mg

CHICKPEA BROCCOLI AND RICE CASSEROLE

GLUTEN-FREE | OIL-FREE | SOY-FREE

SERVES 6 | PREP TIME: 10 minutes | COOK TIME: 30 minutes

This recipe was inspired by Chicken Divan, which is a casserole that's made with chicken, broccoli, and a creamy cheese sauce. It's traditionally served over rice. In this vegan version, hearty chickpeas and broccoli are combined with a healthy, veggie-packed sauce and baked with the rice right in the casserole dish. My Cauliflower Rice (see page 22) can be used instead of brown rice, if you prefer.

6 cups broccoli florets, chopped into bite-size pieces

2 cups cooked brown rice

1 (15-ounce) can chickpeas, drained and rinsed

5 cups Cheesy Vegetable Sauce (see page 24)

Sea salt

Black pepper

Make-ahead tip: I like to make a big pot of brown rice on the weekend, and then freeze it in small containers for meals throughout the week. Typically, rice has a 1:2 ratio to Homemade Vegetable Stock (see page 20) or cooking water. Let the rice cool before freezing it. Some grocery stores carry frozen precooked brown rice, which makes meal-prep even easier.

Per serving: Calories: 313; Total fat: 2g; Total carbs: 44g; Fiber: 12g; Sugar: 7g; Protein: 19g; Sodium: 258mg

1. Preheat your oven to 350°F and have a 9-by-13-inch casserole or baking dish ready.

2. Prepare a large bowl with ice water and bring a large pot of salted water to a boil. Add the broccoli to the boiling water and cook for about 3 minutes, or until the broccoli is bright green. Remove the broccoli from the pot with tongs or a skimmer, and immediately transfer it to the bowl of ice water. Let it sit in the ice water for a minute. Remove the broccoli from the water.

3. Add the broccoli, brown rice, chickpeas, and Cheesy Vegetable Sauce to a large bowl and gently stir to combine. Pour the mixture into the casserole or baking dish. Cover with foil and bake for about 30 minutes, or until the cheese is bubbly. Season with sea salt and black pepper to taste.

Chocolate Avocado Ice Cream, 148

CHAPTER TEN

SWEETS

DATE TRUFFLES

GLUTEN-FREE | LOW-CARB | NUT-FREE OPTION | OIL-FREE | SOY-FREE

MAKES **12 truffles** | PREP TIME: **15 minutes**

There's something indulgent about truffles, but these treats are far from sinful. Just about any type of nuts will work in this recipe. I occasionally make them with pecans or almonds in place of the walnuts. To make them nut-free, use sunflower or pumpkin seeds. Sesame seeds and chocolate complement each other nicely, but you can roll your finished truffles in unsweetened shredded coconut, crushed almonds, or cacao nibs.

½ cup walnuts

1½ cups Medjool dates, pitted

⅓ cup unsweetened, natural cocoa powder

2 teaspoons vanilla extract

¼ teaspoon sea salt

Water

⅓ cup sesame seeds

Ingredient tip: Medjool dates are softer than Deglet Noor dates, so they lend themselves nicely to truffles. They're usually good to go right out of the package, but if they're on the tough side, soak them in water for 15 to 30 minutes. If Medjools aren't available, Deglet Noors can be used, but they should be soaked for 1 to 2 hours before making your truffles. Pat them dry before using them to make the truffles.

Per serving: Calories: 133; Total fat: 6g; Total carbs: 21g; Fiber: 3g; Sugar: 14g; Protein: 3g; Sodium: 45mg

1. Line a baking sheet or platter with parchment paper.

2. Place the walnuts in a food processor and process until they're crumbly. Add the dates, cocoa powder, vanilla extract, and sea salt. Process until everything is well combined and smooth. The mixture should stick together easily. If it's too dry, add some water, 1 tablespoon at a time.

3. Scoop out the mixture by the tablespoonful and roll into small balls, about 1½ inches in diameter. Place them on the prepared baking sheet.

4. Place the sesame seeds in shallow dishes and roll the truffles in them until well coated.

5. Refrigerate the truffles in an airtight container until ready to serve.

STRAWBERRY NICE CREAM

GLUTEN-FREE | LOW-CARB | NUT-FREE OPTION | OIL-FREE | SOY-FREE OPTION

SERVES 4 | PREP TIME: 5 minutes, plus freezing time

Nice cream is a cheerful way of describing ice cream made with a banana base. I first tried it at a 2003 vegan festival in New York City, where a raw food restaurant was serving it in their booth to cool down overheated attendees. I was amazed at how rich and creamy it was, considering it was made almost entirely with frozen bananas and berries. I like to peel and freeze bananas as soon as I get home from the grocery store, so I can make nice cream whenever a craving strikes.

2 bananas, peeled

2 cups strawberries, hulled and halved

¼ cup nondairy milk (such as soy or almond)

1 teaspoon vanilla extract

Substitution tip: Blueberries, raspberries, or cherries can be used in the place of strawberries.

Per serving: Calories: 115; Total fat: 4g; Total carbs: 20g; Fiber: 3g; Sugar: 11g; Protein: 2g; Sodium: 4mg

1. Slice the bananas into small chunks, place them in an airtight container, and then place them in the freezer. Freeze the bananas for 2 to 8 hours. Freezing time will depend on your freezer and how frozen you prefer your ice cream.

2. Place the frozen banana chunks in a blender or food processor along with the strawberries, nondairy milk, and vanilla extract. Process until the mixture is smooth and creamy, scraping down the sides if needed.

3. Serve immediately if you like soft ice cream. If you'd like hard ice cream, transfer the mixture to an airtight container and freeze for 1 to 2 hours, until solid.

CHOCOLATE AVOCADO ICE CREAM

GLUTEN-FREE | NUT-FREE | OIL-FREE | SOY-FREE

SERVES 4 | PREP TIME: 10 minutes, plus freezing time

Much like bananas, avocados blend up smooth and creamy, lending themselves well to nondairy ice cream. Make sure your avocados are ripe because unripe avocados are bitter and won't blend as well. When buying coconut milk, look for full-fat coconut milk in a can. The fat in the coconut milk will keep this ice cream from getting too icy in the freezer. Coconut milk beverage in an aseptic container won't work as well.

3 medium ripe avocados, pitted and sliced

1 cup full-fat coconut milk

¾ cup unsweetened, natural cocoa powder

½ cup plus 2 tablespoons maple syrup

1 tablespoon vanilla extract

½ teaspoon sea salt

Ingredient tip: Natural cocoa powder is the most commonly found cocoa powder in grocery stores. It's made from beans that have been roasted and ground into a powder. Raw cacao powder can also be used in this recipe, but since it is more bitter than natural cocoa powder, you may need to add more maple syrup. Don't confuse cocoa powder with hot cocoa mix because that will not work in this recipe.

Per serving: Calories: 530; Total fat: 37g; Total carbs: 57g; Fiber: 15g; Sugar: 33g; Protein: 7g; Sodium: 212mg

1. Combine avocados, coconut milk, cocoa powder, maple syrup, vanilla extract, and sea salt in a blender or food processor. Process until the mixture is smooth and creamy, scraping down the sides if needed.

2. Pour the mixture into an airtight container and freeze until it's solid. Every freezer is different, but it should take 3 to 4 hours for the mixture to harden.

CHOCOLATE PEANUT BUTTER MOUSSE

GLUTEN-FREE | OIL-FREE

SERVES **6** | PREP TIME: **15 minutes, plus chill time**

I really don't think there's a more dynamic duo than chocolate and peanut butter, and they come together deliciously in this rich mousse. I use the double-boiler method of melting chocolate in this recipe, which only takes a few minutes. Be sure to stir your chocolate chips constantly and remove them from the heat as soon as they've completely melted to ensure that they don't burn.

1 cup nondairy semi-sweet chocolate chips

1 (12-ounce) package silken tofu, drained

1 cup natural creamy peanut butter

½ cup maple syrup

1 teaspoon vanilla extract

½ teaspoon sea salt

Substitution tip: Almond or cashew butter will taste just as delicious as peanut butter in this recipe. Sun butter can be used for those allergic to nuts.

Per serving: Calories: 559; Total fat: 34g; Total carbs: 54g; Fiber: 3g; Sugar: 19g; Protein: 20g; Sodium: 187mg

1. Fill a small saucepan with water and place on the stove over medium heat. Place the chocolate chips in another small saucepan or a heat-proof bowl and place on top of the first saucepan. Stir until the chocolate melts, being careful not to let it burn.

2. Place the melted chocolate into a blender or food processor, along with the tofu, peanut butter, maple syrup, vanilla extract, and sea salt. Process until the mixture is smooth and creamy, stopping to scrape down the sides, if necessary.

3. Refrigerate the mousse for 30 minutes to 1 hour, allowing time for it to firm up slightly.

COOKIE DOUGH BITES

GLUTEN-FREE | LOW-CARB | OIL-FREE | SOY-FREE

MAKES **20 bites** | PREP TIME: **15 minutes,** plus chill time

People know to avoid raw cookie dough when it's made with eggs because of the risk of salmonella, but did you know that the egg-free variety is unsafe, too? Raw flour can harbor bacteria, which can lead to illnesses. This cookie dough is made with chickpeas, rolled oats, and peanut butter, and it is totally safe to consume. In fact, I highly encourage it!

1 (15-ounce) can chickpeas, drained and rinsed

½ cup rolled oats

½ cup natural creamy peanut butter

¼ cup maple syrup

1 teaspoon vanilla extract

½ teaspoon cinnamon

¼ teaspoon sea salt

¼ cup nondairy chocolate chips

Substitution tip: Any type of nut butter can be used in this recipe. Sun butter can be used for those allergic to nuts.

Per serving: Calories: 91; Total fat: 5g; Total carbs: 11g; Fiber: 2g; Sugar: 3g; Protein: 3g; Sodium: 39mg

1. Line a baking sheet or platter with parchment paper.

2. Place the chickpeas, rolled oats, peanut butter, maple syrup, vanilla extract, cinnamon, and sea salt in a food processor and process until smooth and creamy, stopping to scrape down the sides, if necessary. Add the chocolate chips and pulse two or three times to incorporate them into the mixture.

3. Scoop out the mixture by the tablespoonful and roll into small balls, about 1½ inches in diameter. Place them on the prepared baking sheet.

4. Refrigerate the bites for about 30 minutes before serving to allow them to firm up.

OATMEAL ALMOND COOKIES

GLUTEN-FREE | LOW-CARB | OIL-FREE | SOY-FREE

MAKES **16 cookies** | PREP TIME: **10 minutes** | COOK TIME: **12 minutes**

These simple treats only require a few ingredients and a few minutes of your time to make. The batter will be a little soft, but don't worry—the cookies will firm up while baking, as the combination of bananas and almond butter will thicken in the oven. Make sure your bananas are very ripe so that they mash up well.

3 very ripe bananas, peeled

1½ cups rolled oats

½ cup natural creamy almond butter

2 teaspoons cinnamon

1 teaspoon vanilla extract

16 almonds

Substitution tip: Any type of nut butter can be used in this recipe. Sun butter can be used for those allergic to nuts.

Per serving: Calories: 104; Total fat: 5g; Total carbs: 12g; Fiber: 2g; Sugar: 4g; Protein: 3g; Sodium: 17mg

1. Preheat your oven to 350°F and line a baking sheet with parchment paper.

2. Place the bananas into a large bowl and mash them well using a potato masher or large fork.

3. Add the oats, almond butter, cinnamon, and vanilla extract to the bowl and mix well to form a batter.

4. Scoop out the mixture by the tablespoonful and place it on baking sheet in mounds about 2 inches in diameter. Place the mounds about 2 inches apart on your baking sheet. Gently press an almond into each cookie.

5. Bake the cookies for 10 to 12 minutes, or until the edges begin to brown. Remove the cookies from the oven and from the baking sheet and place on a wire rack.

6. Let the cookies cool completely. They will be firmer after they have had time to cool.

MIXED BERRY CRISP

OIL-FREE | SOY-FREE

SERVES 10 | PREP TIME: 10 minutes | COOK TIME: 45 minutes

A crisp is a baked fruit dessert with a crunchy top layer, which is usually made with sugar, nuts, oats, flour, and butter. In this healthy vegan version, I've used almond butter in the place of butter, and maple syrup takes the place of granulated sugar. Serve this crisp warm with a scoop of my Strawberry Nice Cream (see page 147).

16 ounces fresh strawberries, hulled and halved

16 ounces fresh blueberries

6 ounces fresh blackberries

1 cup maple syrup, divided

2 teaspoons cinnamon

2 cups rolled oats

1 cup whole-wheat (or gluten-free) flour

½ cup almonds, coarsely chopped

½ cup natural creamy almond butter

Substitution tip: If fresh berries aren't in season, use 9 to 10 cups of chopped apples or pears (about 5 medium), or a combination of both. Walnuts, pecans, or sunflower seeds can be used instead of almonds, and cashew butter or sun butter can be used instead of almond butter.

Per serving: Calories: 330; Total fat: 11g; Total carbs: 56g; Fiber: 8g; Sugar: 28g; Protein: 7g; Sodium: 61mg

1. Preheat your oven to 350°F and have a 9-by-13-inch casserole or baking dish ready.

2. Place the berries in a large bowl and gently fold in ½ cup of the maple syrup and the cinnamon. Spread the mixture in the casserole dish.

3. In the same large bowl, mix together the oats, flour, almonds, and the remaining maple syrup. Add the almond butter to the mixture and use a spatula or your hands to mix it into the oat mixture.

4. Carefully spread the oat mixture over the berries. Bake for 30 to 40 minutes, or until the top is golden brown and the fruit mixture is bubbly. Allow the crisp to cool for 10 minutes before serving.

BAKED APPLES

GLUTEN-FREE | OIL-FREE | SOY-FREE

MAKES 4 apples | PREP TIME: 15 minutes | COOK TIME: 45 minutes

Baked apples are probably my favorite autumn dessert. They're incredibly simple to make, and the house smells heavenly while they're baking. And, because they're healthy, they can do double duty as breakfast! Some of the best apples for baking include Jonagold, Honeycrisp, Cortland, Braeburn, Gala, and Fuji. Cooking time varies from type to type, and the size will contribute to the time as well. Start checking your apples after 35 minutes. They're done when they are tender but not too mushy.

4 large apples

¼ cup maple syrup

¼ cup unsweetened applesauce

¼ cup chopped walnuts (or pecans)

¼ cup raisins (or dried cranberries)

1 teaspoon cinnamon

1 cup hot water

Speed it up: Apples can be "baked" in an air fryer. Pop them in the air fryer basket and cook them on 375°F for 18 to 22 minutes, or until they're tender.

Per serving: Calories: 251; Total fat: 6g; Total carbs: 54g; Fiber: 7g; Sugar: 42g; Protein: 2g; Sodium: 5mg

1. Preheat your oven to 375°F and have an 8-by-8-inch baking dish ready.

2. Use a sharp knife or apple corer to remove the cores of the apples. Create a well that's about ¾-inch wide and leave about half an inch at the bottom of each apple.

3. In a medium bowl, mix together the maple syrup, applesauce, walnuts, raisins, and cinnamon. Spoon the mixture evenly into each apple.

4. Pour the water into the baking dish. Then place the apples, containing the spooned mixture, into the baking dish and bake them for 35 to 45 minutes, or until the apples are tender.

KEY LIME BARS

MAKES **12 bars** | PREP TIME: **15 minutes** | COOK TIME: **30 minutes**

Key limes get their name from the Florida Keys; they're smaller and have a more intense flavor than the regular variety. They were originally grown in the West Indies and were brought to Florida by Spanish explorers, where they thrived in the hot, humid weather. Limes are a good source of vitamins C and B6, as well as potassium, folic acid, and the phytochemical limonene. I've added a handful of spinach to this recipe for color as well as a nutrient boost.

1½ cups almonds

10 Medjool dates, pitted

¼ cup shredded coconut

½ teaspoon sea salt

1 (12-ounce) package silken tofu

1 ripe banana, peeled

1 cup spinach, packed

½ cup key lime juice

½ cup agave

¼ cup cornstarch (or arrowroot)

Ingredient tip: I like to use bottled Key lime juice when making this recipe because juicing limes can be messy and time-consuming. Regular lime juice can be used if key lime juice isn't available.

Per serving: Calories: 312; Total fat: 11g; Total carbs: 53g; Fiber: 7g; Sugar: 37g; Protein: 7g; Sodium: 100mg

1. Preheat your oven to 350°F and line an 8-by-8-inch baking dish with parchment paper.

2. Place the almonds, dates, coconut, and sea salt in a food processor and pulse until the mixture resembles crumbs. Press the mixture into the bottom of the prepared baking dish.

3. Place the silken tofu, banana, spinach, key lime juice, agave, and cornstarch into a food processor or blender and blend until smooth and creamy, scraping down the sides if necessary.

4. Pour the tofu mixture on top of the crust. Bake for 30 minutes, or until the center has completely set, or until a toothpick inserted in the center comes out clean.

5. Allow the bars to cool completely, and then wrap the baking dish tightly and refrigerate it for at least 2 hours. Slice into 12 bars.

SWEET POTATO BROWNIES

GLUTEN-FREE OPTION | LOW-CARB | NUT-FREE OPTION | OIL-FREE | SOY-FREE OPTION

MAKES **18 brownies** | PREP TIME: **10 minutes** | COOK TIME: **25 minutes**

There's some debate about how brownies should taste. Should they be fudgy or cakey? I can never pick a side because I like both. These brownies fall into the cakey category. No one will guess that their moist texture comes from sweet potatoes. Pumpkin purée can be used instead of sweet potato purée for an autumn-themed treat. Serve these brownies warm with a scoop of my Strawberry Nice Cream (see page 147) or Chocolate Avocado Ice Cream (see page 148).

1 (15-ounce) can sweet potato purée (or 1 medium sweet potato, baked or steamed)

¾ cup nondairy milk (such as soy or almond)

½ cup maple syrup

2 teaspoons vanilla extract

2 cups whole-wheat (or all-purpose gluten-free) flour mix

½ cup Dutch cocoa powder

1½ teaspoons baking powder

1 teaspoon cinnamon

½ teaspoon baking soda

½ teaspoon sea salt

Ingredient tip: Dutch cocoa powder is treated with an alkali and is less acidic than natural cocoa powder. It has a mellow flavor and dissolves easily in liquids.

Per serving: Calories: 96; Total fat: 1g; Total carbs: 21g; Fiber: 2g; Sugar: 6g; Protein: 2g; Sodium: 107mg

1. Preheat your oven to 350°F and line a 9-by-13-inch baking dish with parchment paper.

2. In a medium bowl, whisk together the sweet potato purée, nondairy milk, maple syrup, and vanilla extract.

3. In a large bowl, mix together the flour, cocoa powder, baking powder, cinnamon, baking soda, and sea salt. Pour the wet ingredients into the bowl and mix until everything is well-combined.

4. Pour the mixture into the prepared baking dish, spreading the mixture evenly. Bake the brownies for 20 to 25 minutes, or until a toothpick inserted in the center comes out clean.

5. Allow the brownies to cool completely before slicing into 18 bars.

PREP AND COOK VEGETABLE CHART

VEGETABLE	HOW TO PREPARE IT	COOKING METHOD	BEST WAY TO EAT
ASPARAGUS	Trim ends	Blanched, roasted, sautéed	Salads, pasta dishes
BELL PEPPERS	Remove stem and seeds	Raw, roasted, baked	Sauces, soups, stuffed with vegetables
BRUSSELS SPROUTS	Trim bottoms	Sautéed, roasted, broiled, raw	Salads
BUTTERNUT SQUASH	Peel, remove seeds	Roasted, boiled, puréed	Salads, soups, sauces
CARROTS	Peel	Raw, boiled, roasted	Salads, soups
CAULIFLOWER	Remove outer leaves	Broiled, roasted, riced, steamed	Soups and stews, stir-fries, tacos
EDAMAME	Shell or keep in pods	Steamed, boiled	Stir-fries, salads
EGGPLANT	Remove stem	Roasted, broiled, simmered	Soups and stews, stuffed with vegetables
GREEN BEANS	Trim ends	Blanched, roasted, sautéed, stir-fried	Salads, stir-fries
KALE	Remove stems, massage leaves	Raw, sautéed	Salads, soups
SWEET POTATO	Scrub skin	Roasted	Fries, salads
ZUCCHINI	Trim ends	Shaved into noodles, sautéed, roasted	Substitute for pasta, soups and stews, fries

PRODUCE STORAGE GUIDE

Don't let those vegetables go bad! Proper storage will help your produce stay fresh longer, which means less waste and less money spent at the grocery store. Here are some tips and tricks for keeping produce fresh:

Asparagus stalks should be kept wet to keep them fresh. You can trim the stalks and place them upright in a glass of fresh water, or you can wrap the ends in a damp paper towel. Be sure to replace the water or damp towel every day or two.

Unripe avocados should be stored at room temperature on a counter, where they will last up to seven days. The ripening process can be hastened by placing them in a paper bag. Once avocados are ripe, they can be stored in the fruit drawer of your refrigerator.

Both **beets and radishes,** without their greens attached, will last up to a month in the refrigerator. Store them in a loose or perforated bag in the vegetable drawer of your refrigerator. If their greens are attached, they will last three to five days.

Bell peppers will last in the vegetable drawer of the refrigerator for about a week.

Broccoli should be kept in a sealed bag in the vegetable drawer of your refrigerator.

Brussels sprouts and **cauliflower** should be kept in loose or perforated bags in the vegetable drawer of your refrigerator.

Cabbage should be stored in a sealed bag in the vegetable drawer of your refrigerator.

Carrots will stay fresh for long periods of time in cold temperatures. Store them in the coldest place in the refrigerator wrapped in a towel or in a loose or perforated bag.

Celery can be stored in a sealed container or bag in the refrigerator.

Eggplants are delicate and can lose their freshness quickly. Store them in a sealed bag in the vegetable drawer of your refrigerator.

Delicate herbs like parsley and cilantro should be stored unwashed in a loose bag in the refrigerator. Heartier herbs like basil and rosemary should be stored in the refrigerator wrapped in a damp paper towel.

Leafy greens, such as kale, collard greens, and lettuce should be wrapped in a damp towel or loose bag and placed in the crisper drawer of your refrigerator. Don't wash your greens before storing them or they will wilt too quickly.

Winter squash, potatoes, sweet potatoes, onions, and garlic don't need to be refrigerated. They can be stored in a cool, dark place, such as a pantry or cupboard. Don't store potatoes and onions next to each other because the gases they each emit will cause the other to rot.

Zucchini and summer squash should be stored unwashed in a loose or perforated bag in the vegetable drawer of the refrigerator.

THE DIRTY DOZEN™ AND THE CLEAN FIFTEEN™

A nonprofit environmental watchdog organization called Environmental Working Group (EWG) looks at data supplied by the US Department of Agriculture (USDA) and the Food and Drug Administration (FDA) about pesticide residues. Each year it compiles a list of the best and worst pesticide loads found in commercial crops. You can use these lists to decide which fruits and vegetables to buy organic to minimize your exposure to pesticides and which produce is considered safe enough to buy conventionally. This does not mean they are pesticide-free, though, so wash these fruits and vegetables thoroughly. The list is updated annually, and you can find it online at EWG.org/FoodNews.

DIRTY DOZEN™

1. strawberries
2. spinach
3. kale
4. nectarines
5. apples
6. grapes
7. peaches
8. cherries
9. pears
10. tomatoes
11. celery
12. potatoes

†Additionally, nearly three-quarters of hot pepper samples contained pesticide residues.

CLEAN FIFTEEN™

1. avocados
2. sweet corn*
3. pineapples
4. sweet peas (frozen)
5. onions
6. papayas*
7. eggplants
8. asparagus
9. kiwis
10. cabbages
11. cauliflower
12. cantaloupes
13. broccoli
14. mushrooms
15. honeydew melons

* A small amount of sweet corn, papaya, and summer squash sold in the United States is produced from genetically modified seeds. Buy organic varieties of these crops if you want to avoid genetically modified produce.

MEASUREMENT CONVERSIONS

	US STANDARD	US STANDARD (OUNCES)	METRIC (APPROXIMATE)
VOLUME EQUIVALENTS (LIQUID)	2 tablespoons	1 fl. oz.	30 mL
	¼ cup	2 fl. oz.	60 mL
	½ cup	4 fl. oz.	120 mL
	1 cup	8 fl. oz.	240 mL
	1½ cups	12 fl. oz.	355 mL
	2 cups or 1 pint	16 fl. oz.	475 mL
	4 cups or 1 quart	32 fl. oz.	1 L
	1 gallon	128 fl. oz.	4 L
VOLUME EQUIVALENTS (DRY)	⅛ teaspoon	———	0.5 mL
	¼ teaspoon	———	1 mL
	½ teaspoon	———	2 mL
	¾ teaspoon	———	4 mL
	1 teaspoon	———	5 mL
	1 tablespoon	———	15 mL
	¼ cup	———	59 mL
	⅓ cup	———	79 mL
	½ cup	———	118 mL
	⅔ cup	———	156 mL
	¾ cup	———	177 mL
	1 cup	———	235 mL
	2 cups or 1 pint	———	475 mL
	3 cups	———	700 mL
	4 cups or 1 quart	———	1 L
	½ gallon	———	2 L
	1 gallon	———	4 L
WEIGHT EQUIVALENTS	½ ounce	———	15 g
	1 ounce	———	30 g
	2 ounces	———	60 g
	4 ounces	———	115 g
	8 ounces	———	225 g
	12 ounces	———	340 g
	16 ounces or 1 pound	———	455 g

	FAHRENHEIT (F)	CELSIUS (C) (APPROXIMATE)
OVEN TEMPERATURES	250°F	120°F
	300°F	150°C
	325°F	180°C
	375°F	190°C
	400°F	200°C
	425°F	220°C
	450°F	230°C

REFERENCES

Barnard, Neal, M.D. *Food for Life: How the New Four Food Groups Can Save Your Life*. New York: Harmony, 1993.

Costigan, Fran. *Vegan Chocolate: Unapologetically Luscious and Decadent Dairy-Free Desserts*. Philadelphia: Running Press, 2013.

Davis, Brenda, and Vesanto Melina. *Becoming Vegan Express Edition: The Everyday Guide to Plant-based Nutrition*. Completely revised edition. Summertown: Book Publishing Company, 2013.

Fuhrman, Joel, M.D. *Eat to Live: The Revolutionary Formula for Fast and Sustained Weight Loss*. New York: Little, Brown and Company, 2003.

Greger, Michael, M.D., and Gene Stone. *How Not to Die: Discover the Foods Scientifically Proven to Prevent and Reverse Disease*. New York: Flatiron Books, 2015.

Hever, Julieanna, and Raymond J. Cronise. *Plant-Based Nutrition (Idiot's Guide)*. Second edition. New York: DK Publishing, 2018.

Mateljan, George. *The World's Healthiest Foods: Essential Guide for the Healthiest Way of Eating*. Seattle: GMF Publishing, 2006.

Messina, Virginia, and JL Fields. *Vegan for Her: The Woman's Guide to Being Healthy and Fit on a Plant-Based Diet*. Philadelphia: Da Capo Press, 2013.

Murry, Michael, Joseph Pizzorno, and Lara Pizzorno. *The Encyclopedia of Healing Foods*. New York: Atria Books, 2005.

Reynolds, Andrew, et al. "Carbohydrate Quality and Human Health: A Series of Systematic Reviews and Meta-Analyses." *The Lancet* 393, no. 10170 (January 10, 2019): 434-45. https://doi.org/10.1016/S0140-6736(18)31809-9.

INDEX

ACKNOWLEDGMENTS

I couldn't have written this book without the support of Dennis Mason, who tested recipes, washed dishes, and made emergency trips to the grocery store for supplies. Thank you for everything!

I'm forever grateful to my recipe testers: Jennifer Smith and Sadie Smith; Ruth Schlomer and Mike Sojkowski; Eileen Mallor; Karyn Gost; Donna M. Kaminski, her family, and coworkers; Marissa Strauss with helpers Emma and Hannah; and Dana Holmes. Thank you all so much for your help!

Thank you so much to my friends and family for your support, especially my dad, Bill Wenz. Fran Costigan, I'm so thankful for your words of wisdom and support with this project.

I'm eternally thankful to Jessica Caneal for encouraging me to start a blog back in 2009. Thank you to all of the blog readers who visit my website and cook up my recipes. I'm so grateful for the support of my friends in the vegan blogging community. Special thanks to Cadry Nelson for listening when I needed to talk.

And, of course, thank you so much to the team at Callisto Media, especially Michael Goodman, for entrusting me with this project.

ABOUT THE AUTHOR

 Dianne Wenz is a Certified Holistic Health Coach, vegan lifestyle coach, plant-based chef, and has a certificate in plant-based nutrition. Dianne coaches people from across the globe, supporting them in improving their health and well-being, as well as making the dietary and lifestyle changes needed to go vegan. She teaches both private and public cooking classes in northern New Jersey. She is also the editor-in-chief of ChicVegan.com.

Dianne lives in New Jersey with her partner, Dennis Mason, and their cats, Archie, Clementine, Tallulah Belle, and Rupert.

Visit DiannesVeganKitchen.com for healthy living tips, nutrition information, and recipes.

CPSIA information can be obtained
at www.ICGtesting.com
Printed in the USA
LVHW012023071219
639669LV00002B/2/P

9 781646 112272